SEA KAYAK
NAVIGATION

Franco Ferrero

A PRACTICAL MANUAL

First published 1999
Second edition 2007

Published in Great Britain 2007 by Pesda Press
Unit 22, Galeri
Doc Victoria
Caernarfon
Gwynedd
LL55 1SQ

ISBN: 978–1–906095–03–1

Printed in Poland, produced by Polskabook.

To Joan, my guiding star.

THE AUTHOR
Franco Ferrero

Franco began sea kayaking at the age of fifteen, and was lucky enough to be brought up in the Channel Islands. The small scattered islands, fast tidal streams and summer fogs ensured that navigation was a key skill learnt at an early age.

In 1978 he was one of a team of three Jerseymen who completed the first circumnavigation of Ireland by sea kayak. In 1989, with Kevin Danforth, he made a record breaking unsupported crossing of the North Sea. Since then he has paddled in many parts of the world including Nepal, Scandinavia, the coast of Brittany in France, the European Alps, Peru and Western Canada.

He is the managing director of Pesda Press and still occasionally manages to fit in some freelance coaching (as a BCU Level 5 Coach). He lives in Wales, escaping the office to go sea and whitewater kayaking, rock and ice climbing, and ski-mountaineering. His current passion is a twenty-nine foot yacht called 'Firebird'.

INTRODUCTION

The aim of this book is to provide a concise manual of navigation aimed specifically at sea kayakers. In this respect this second edition is no different from the first.

There is no glossary of terms as things are explained as I go along. To compensate there is a comprehensive index.

The devil is in the detail. Feedback from readers of the first edition has changed my views on 'what sea kayakers need to know and are likely to use'. I have added to several topics, but have taken care to keep it short and simple.

Using the book

Each chapter ends with a number of suggested exercises. Make use of them – they will help to ensure that what you have read is understood and remembered.

EXERCISES

Check your answers to each of the exercises at: pesdapress.com/answers

The ultimate test of whether or not the lessons have been absorbed is the first time you plan and execute a trip relying on your own navigation. Be cautious; plan simple trips and aim for big targets to start with.

The illustrations and diagrams throughout the book are available to download as a teaching resource four use in your slideshow presentations at pesdapress.com/ presentations

Ask someone more experienced to check your calculations the first few times. Get someone else on the trip to make independent plans and compare your results. If they are a near match, carry on – if they disagree, start again!

Always take into account the weather forecast, and base your planning on the abilities of the weakest members of your group.

Build up slowly.

Enjoy the book and enjoy your paddling.

ACKNOWLEDGEMENTS

I would like to thank Danny Finton, Danny Jones, Joan Ferrero, Trys Morris, Nigel Robinson, Olly Sanders and Bob Timms for their help with the first edition.

For their help with the second edition, I would like to thank: Nigel Robinson for suggesting and giving examples of the exercises that are now to be found at the end of each chapter; Andy Stamp, with his impressive knowledge of both the theory and practice of navigating using GPS, who suggested numerous improvements to that chapter; Kevin Mansell, whose practical experience of GPS led to a number of improvements; Gordon Brown who, drawing on his vast experience, suggested numerous improvements throughout the book; Mike Mclure and Oisin Hallissey whose work on developing a BCU Coastal Navigation and Tidal Planning modules pointed out a couple of omissions. Peter Wood for help with the photography and the new design of this edition.

Finally, a special thanks is due to Bill Ayles who introduced me to the delights of navigation theory and Dave Thelland who first helped me to use it for sea kayaking.

Photographic Acknowledgements

A special thank you is due to the people who allowed me to use their photographs. I'd also like to thank those people who sent photos that I didn't end up using. Unless indicated below, all photos were taken by Franco Ferrero or Peter Wood.

Jeff Allen p14; Doug Cooper, p51, p96 (title); Joan Ferrero p42; Derek Hairon p13; Laurie Bell iStockphoto.com p15; Howard Jeffs p96 (inset); Kevin Mansell p77; Douglas Wilcox p29, p67, p90.

CONTENTS

Port Argus

Cross

Broken Head

beacon
Bonecrusher Rock

Following the coast and using
obvious features to keep track
of your position on the chart.

1 KEEPING IT SIMPLE

Ask yourself if you need to do any chart work. If you are paddling across to a small island that is out of sight, your chart work will need to be precise. On the other hand if you are 10 nautical miles out to sea off the west coast of the United States, it may be quite accurate enough to head due east (090°) until you sight land; and then work out precisely where you are when you get there.

MAP & CHART SYMBOLS

Maps and charts aimed at leisure users have a 'legend' or 'key' that shows you what symbols are used to indicate various features. We will look at maps and charts in detail in Chapter 4.

Handrails

Let's not forget that "turn left and follow the coastline until you get there" is often quite appropriate! The coastline itself provides the 'handrail' for you to follow. Keeping track of your position is done by simply 'ticking off' prominent features as you pass them by. These features are anything that is easy to recognise on the chart and in the real world. They could be natural features such as sea stacks, isolated rocks, inlets and prominent points, or man made features such as buoys, radio masts and prominent buildings.

JUDGING DISTANCE

A simple way to estimate distance is to gauge how much detail you can make out. Below is the resolvable detail method from *Sea Kayak* by Gordon Brown.

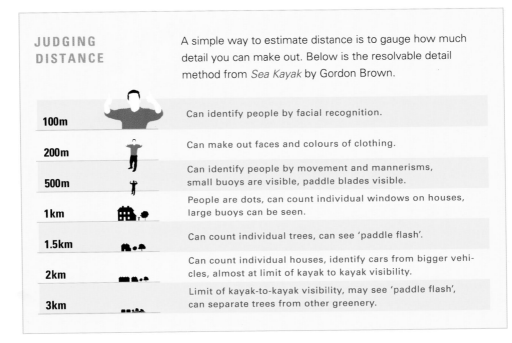

100m	Can identify people by facial recognition.
200m	Can make out faces and colours of clothing.
500m	Can identify people by movement and mannerisms, small buoys are visible, paddle blades visible.
1km	People are dots, can count individual windows on houses, large buoys can be seen.
1.5km	Can count individual trees, can see 'paddle flash'.
2km	Can count individual houses, identify cars from bigger vehicles, almost at limit of kayak to kayak visibility.
3km	Limit of kayak-to-kayak visibility, may see 'paddle flash', can separate trees from other greenery.

Eyeball navigation

Even if you are not following a handrail it is often best to find your way and keep track of your position by working your way from one clearly visible feature to the next. This is what sailors call 'pilotage'.

1   On a land map that covers a coastal area, find the symbols for and examples of the following features:

A lighthouse.
A beacon (like a small lighthouse without a light).
A cliff.
Rocky shoreline.
Sand.
Sand dunes.
Shingle (shoreline).
Mud (shoreline).

2   Take your own map or chart on the next coastal sea kayak journey you go on. See how many prominent features you can identify on the map or chart as you paddle.

3   Before your next journey, study the route on the chart and note how many points you can identify that you think you will see along the coast. Then tick them off as you paddle.

2 DECKTOP NAVIGATION

Above ~ a kayaker's
'chart table' and equipment.

One of the problems of navigating in a sea kayak is that we don't have the luxury of being able to go below, consult the pilot, or plot a new course on a full size chart table. We have to compensate for this in three ways:

1. Doing as much chart work as possible before going afloat.

2. Adapting our navigation equipment.

3. Choosing the simplest solutions.

Passage planning

Passage planning is the term used for all the gathering of information, planning and chart work that can take place before you start a journey. Due to the fact that tides can usually be accurately predicted, it is possible to do all the tidal planning and necessary corrections from the comfort of your living room. All you then have to do is make sure you set off precisely on time and, if necessary, make allowances for the effect of the wind or unusual conditions.

Equipment

The equipment has to be adapted to protect it from the effects of salt water, and make it practical for use on the small area of deck that is forward of the cockpit and within reach.

The deck

The deck is your chart table. It can be made more effective by:

- Fitting a number of elastic cords to hold your charts in place.

- Sticking some white sticky back plastic onto the deck on which you can write information that you might need during the voyage.

- Fixing a deck bag in front of your 'chart table' in which to keep your plotting instruments and other equipment.

- Taping a light stick to the deck so as to illuminate your compass on night paddles, and keeping a head torch handy.

For my deck bag I use a bum bag (fanny pack) which I can carry with me away from the boat.

Charts & maps

Charts and maps can be cut into conveniently sized sections and laminated in plastic. Before laminating, care must be taken to ensure that:

- Relevant information is copied onto the chart so that you don't need to consult reference books.

- The chart is cut so that each section has a latitude and longitude scale, or this information is transferred.

- The tidal information boxes are cut out and glued onto the same piece of chart that contains the diamond to which the box refers (See Predicting Tides, page 55).

- Extra latitude and longitude lines are drawn in if they are too widely spaced on your chart. On other maps such as British Ordnance Survey Landrangers, the grid lines are fine for our purposes.

TOP TIP

Don't cut down your charts and maps too much. It is better to have to fold a map than to run off the edge of a cut-down one several times in a journey.

Waterproof map cases are a good alternative to cutting and laminating your charts. These are very practical for sit-on-top kayaks which have no deck on which to keep laminates! Go for the largest size you can get; it is better to fold the map case than to have to take the chart out and re-fold it.

Plotting instruments

I recommend carrying the following course plotting instruments (how to use these and other instruments is explained later):

- A large mountaineering style compass to measure the angles when laying off (plotting) courses.

- A 30cm (12 inch) ruler for drawing lines and measuring distances off the chart. A folding one, as shown, is great.

- A waterproof notepad.

- Ordinary lead pencils, Chinagraph pencils (grease pencils) and fine permanent markers.

The compass lanyard, can also be used for measuring distances.

A kayaker's decktop plotting instruments.

SQUARE PLOTTER

With the addition of a piece of string tied through the centre, a square plotter becomes a versatile instrument for measuring, drawing and laying off courses. You might find it a useful replacement for the compass and ruler when plotting your trip.

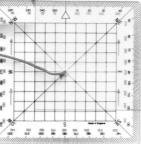

I had dismissed the square plotter as difficult to use; thanks to Jeff Allen for showing me how to improve them with a simple length of string.

CHECKLIST

Write yourself a checklist of essential paddling kit and add to it all the items listed under 'plotting instruments' – make sure you carry them all. This is where a removable deck bag really helps you stay organised.

3 TIDES

Anyone who has been to the seaside knows that the sea comes in, washes away your sand castles, and then goes out, leaving you with a long walk to the water's edge.

High & low water

Members of the Flat Earth Society may as well stop reading at this point!

Tides are caused mainly by the gravitational pull of the moon. Imagine that the earth is a sphere covered in an even layer of water. The pull of the moon causes the water to bulge towards it; to balance things out there is a roughly equal bulge on the other side of the earth. The result is that in our example, at 0600 hours, we have high water (HW) and because the earth does one complete rotation on its axis every 24 hours, in just over six hours time it is low water (LW).

The bulges either side of the globe correspond to two high waters every day. On Monday HW occurs at six o'clock in the morning and evening.

TUESDAY

MONDAY

NORTH POLE

0600
0700
0800
0900
1000
1100
1200
1300
1400
1500
1600
1700
1800
1900
2000
2100
2200
2300
2400
2500
2600
2700
2800
2900

TIME OF DAY

The two bulges correspond to two HWs and two LWs in 24 hours – a **semi-diurnal** tidal pattern (the most common type). However, high and low water are not exactly six hours apart every day, the period is a little longer. This is because, while the earth spins, the moon is also orbiting the earth. Page 15 shows low water at mid-day on Monday, but on Tuesday low water is nearly an hour later.

If you are paddling in a part of the world that doesn't fit the semi-diurnal model you will have to adjust the times to fit your pattern.

Arriving at the coast at 10.00 a.m. we notice that the tide has reached its high point, so we can tell that for the next six hours, until 4.00 p.m. the tide will be going down. This rough guide is usually good enough for a sea kayaker's needs.

Tidal patterns

Because the world isn't covered evenly in water, the differing sizes of the oceans and the effects of oscillation – semi-diurnal tides aren't the only pattern found in the world. There are also **diurnal** and **mixed** tides.

Diurnal, semi-diurnal and mixed tide patterns and their worldwide distribution.

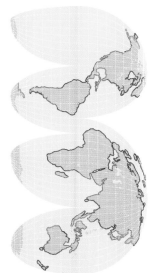

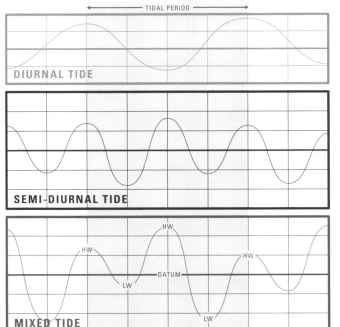

ANOMALOUS TIDES

Not all places have tides that follow the pattern described above. Semi-diurnal tides that don't follow the 6 hour pattern usually occur where the shape of the coastline is complex – a maze of islands or an enclosed body of water. It may be that the flood is longer or shorter than the ebb, for example the tide might rise for seven hours and fall for five. Where the geography is unusual, study your sources of tidal information **carefully**.

A famous example occurs in the Solent (between the Isle of Wight and the south coast of England). Here the water rises to high water, drops for a while and then briefly rises again before finally dropping to low water – in effect two high waters!
(I prefer to think of it as one false high water and one real one).

An unusual tidal curve for the area between Lymington and Yarmouth. Tides are usually described in terms of hours before or after HW; here the curve is depicted in terms of hours before and after LW. This is because in this almost unique case there are two high waters but only one low water.

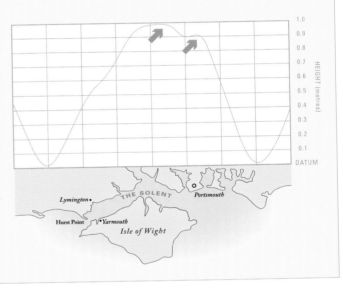

To yachtsmen and mariners, the prospect of running aground at low tide is a serious one.

To kayakers whether the tide is high or low is rarely crucial from a navigational point of view. Low water may make estuaries unpaddleable or might mean a long tiring carry up a beach at the end of the day. What does affect us more than other craft (because we are relatively slow) are tidal streams (the horizontal flow of water caused by tidal movement).

Flood & ebb

The period between low water and high water, when the water level rises, is known as the flood. The period from high water to low water, when the water level goes down, is known as the ebb.

Tidal movement

The rise and fall of the tide varies immensely from place to place. Tides are not uniform because the surface of the Earth is irregular. In a large ocean basin like the North Atlantic, the tides oscillate back and forth much like the tea in your cup when you nearly spill it, producing maximum vertical movement at the edges. If you paddle on the Atlantic west coast of Ireland you will find that the tide moves up and down by anything up to 10m whereas in the Azores the tidal rise and fall is much smaller.

The larger the mass of water the greater the effect of the gravitational pull of the moon.

Tidal oscillation in the oceans.

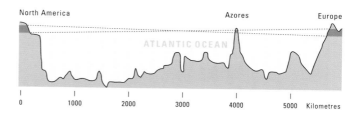

Flow of water into the Irish Sea.

Tidal streams

Despite the large tidal range, there is very little horizontal movement of water on the west coast of Ireland. However the Irish Sea is such a small body of water that, were it land locked, it would hardly rise and fall at all. It does have a rise and fall because water pours in and out from and to the Atlantic, a horizontal movement of water. These horizontal movements of water are what we call tidal streams. Tidal streams often flow as fast as a kayak can travel (in some places faster), so it is essential that we use them rather than fight them.

Tidal range

To properly understand and predict tidal streams we must take a closer look at tidal rise and fall because the power of tidal streams is directly influenced by the amount of vertical movement.

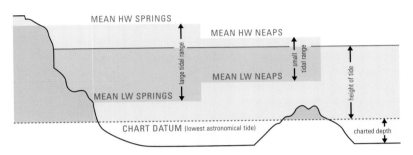

Tidal range. Tidal heights are measured from the chart datum (lowest astronomical tide).

The difference in height between LW and HW is known as the tidal range. The tidal range changes daily due to the effects of the sun and moon. The moon, the closest astronomical body to the earth, has the greatest effect upon tides. The sun, much more massive but so much further away, has a lesser but noticeable effect.

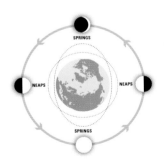

Springs

When the sun and the moon are in line they work together. Therefore at new moon, and again 14 days later at full moon, the tides are at their greatest; these are known as spring tides. The word 'spring' has nothing to do with the season, it is a Viking word that means 'a lack of' and refers to the fact that at low tides the water goes down a lot further than usual and is still a favourite time for yachtsmen to run aground.

Lunar phases determine spring and neap tides.

Neaps

The opposite occurs when the moon and the sun work against each other. The moon still has the greater effect so the water still bulges towards the moon. However, as the sun is pulling in the other direction, the bulge is reduced and the tide does not rise as high or fall as low. These are known as neap tides. Neap is also a Viking word and it means 'an abundance' of water because at low water there is still plenty of water under your longship. The moon takes one lunar month (about 27 days) to orbit the Earth so there is about a week between springs and neaps.

EQUINOCTIAL TIDES

The highest tides with the greatest tidal range occur at the spring tide nearest the equinox. The equinox is when the sun is directly over the equator and has the greatest gravitational pull on the Earth. This occurs around the 21st of March and the 23rd of September and the two occurrences are known as the spring and autumn (or fall) equinoxes.

The effect of springs and neaps on tidal streams

The tidal range at springs is about twice that of neaps. This means that in most places (unless your sources of tidal information tell you otherwise) it is safe to assume that the speed of the tidal stream is half as fast at neaps as it is at springs.

So if the speed of the tidal stream at a given point in the cycle (say for example 1 hour after HW) is 1 knot, then at the same point in the cycle (1 hour after HW) at neaps the speed will be 0.5 knots. Half way between springs and neaps it will be 0.75.

Tidal stream behaviour

Close inshore the tidal streams generally follow the coast. Where the coastline is straightforward the tidal stream will usually flow in one direction for about 6 hours, have a short period of slack and then flow the other way. The periods of slack water don't necessarily coincide with local high water and low water. For this reason, pilots always refer to the direction of flow rather than ebb and flood.

There will be further explanation of this in Chapter 10 Predicting Tides.

Wherever there are complications such as numerous islands and channels, bodies of water with multiple entrances, or different ocean basins meeting each other, the periods of flow and times of slack water may vary considerably. Here you will have to rely on your personal observation or careful study of the tidal information.

WEATHER CONDITIONS

Tide table predictions are based on average atmospheric pressure. Exceptionally high or low pressure can change the predicted height of the tide, the times of high and low water and the resulting times and speeds of the tidal streams.

EXERCISES

1 Answer the following questions (The answers are all in the chapter. Go back over it until you can answer the questions. If you wish to check your answers they can be found at www.pesdapress.com/answers):

A Is the tidal pattern found in Europe diurnal or semi-diurnal?

B If HW is 8.6m and LW is 1.0m, what is the tidal range?

C If the tidal range at springs is 6m, what would you expect it to be at neaps?

D You observe that on a spring tide, two hours after HW, the tidal stream is running at 4 knots. How fast will the tidal stream run in the same location, two hours after HW, on a tide with a range that is halfway between springs and neaps?

2 Explain to someone else the meaning of: **ebb**, **flood**, **tidal stream**, **spring tide**, **neap tide** and **tidal range**. If you are able to do this, you really understand the terms.

4 MAPS & CHARTS

In order to navigate in strange places and over large distances we need to use some form of map. The two choices are nautical charts or land maps.

Charts

Nautical charts only show the land detail that is visible from the sea. This is great when you are on the water, but useless when you have to make an unforeseen landing because of changing weather and are trying to find the quickest way back to your vehicle. They do, however, have several definite advantages:

1. They show the shape and depth of the seabed, which may enable you to make educated guesses about sea conditions or tides where there is not much information available.

2. They show the position of buoys and details of any lights (useful on night paddles, planned or accidental).

3. They give tidal information.

British Admiralty and US National Ocean Service charts are similarly colour coded which makes things easy. Yellow areas are dry land, green bits are covered in water at high tide and dry (or very shallow) at low tide. White and blue bits are always underwater.

Yachtsmen's charts produced by firms such as Imray may differ in colour coding, but the principles are the same.

Standard charts for shipping are large and unfolded but there are also more convenient 'Leisure Series' charts designed for use by yachtsmen. These are often in useful scales, so that you only need one chart instead of three or four overlapping charts, and they come in folded and unfolded versions.

Maps

The main advantage of land maps is that many people are already familiar with them.

Land maps have the advantage of showing all land details, including such essentials as pubs, public toilets, access roads and paths. They show all coastal features, including anything that shows at low water. On the other hand, they don't show buoys, lights (except lighthouses) or any features of the seabed (below the low water mark).

Scale

UNITS

A nautical mile (NM) is slightly greater than one land mile (1.15 to be precise), and is roughly equivalent to 2km. 1 knot (kn) = 1 nautical mile per hour. It is easier to work in nautical miles, rather than miles or kilometres, because all tidal information is given in knots.

Small Scale (1:1,000 where 1cm on the map = 1,000cm or 10m on the ground). A small ratio means lots of detail but you'll need an awful lot of maps. These are usually used to provide detail of harbours and are seldom of use to kayakers.

Large Scale (1:1,000,000 where 1cm on the map = 1,000,000cm or 10km on the ground). A map of this scale would cover the whole west coast of Ireland (great for planning, but no use for day-to-day navigation).

I find the most useful scales to be between these two extremes 1:50,000 or 1:100,000 for both charts and land maps.

Comparison of Ordnance Survey Landranger map and Admiralty Leisure Series chart styles
(both 1:50,000 scale). OS maps also have a latitude scale along the outer edge of the sheet.

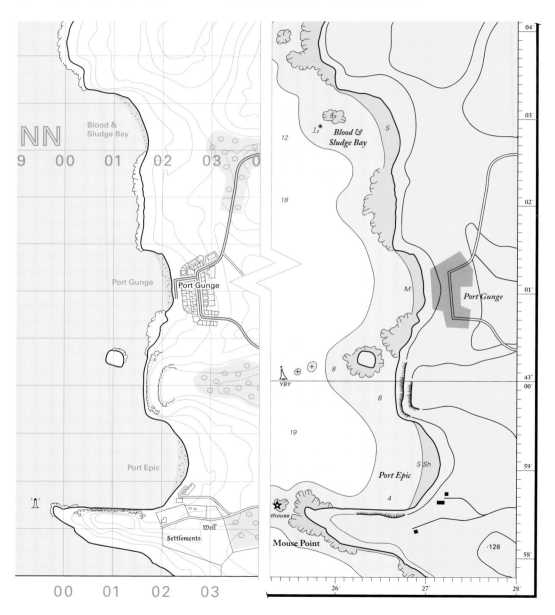

Measuring distance

To measure a distance on a map or chart, I suggest either a pair of dividers (looks professional, especially the expensive brass ones, preserves mystique, are slightly more accurate and are easier to use on the kitchen table), or a piece of string (cheaper and easier to use when afloat). Simply open the dividers to the required distance and then measure off against the latitude scale which you will find at either edge of the chart.

> 1 minute (1') of latitude = 1 nautical mile (NM)
> 1° = 60 minutes or 60NM

A pair of dividers or a piece of string will be useful for taking measurements from the diagrams in this book.

Consequently, on the example chart opposite, the distance from Blood and Sludge Bay to Port Epic is 4NM (or 4' of latitude).

LATITUDE AND LONGITUDE

The earth is a sphere. (It's actually slightly squashed at the poles but for the purposes of navigation we can ignore that). Lines of **Latitude** begin at 0°, bisecting the globe around the Equator and slice the globe into rings at regular intervals toward each of the poles. Degrees of latitude are measured from the centre of the Earth, north and south of the Equator.

Lines of **Longitude** are drawn bisecting the globe from pole to pole at angles east or west of what is known as the Prime Meridian, or 0° of longitude (this could be anywhere but historically the line runs through the Greenwich Observatory, Great Britain). Lines of longitude converge at the poles (think of the segments of an orange). Thus a minute of longitude becomes progressively smaller in terms of distance as you go towards the poles. For this reason we do not use longitude for measuring distance.

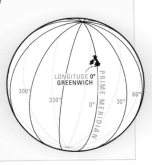

MAP PROJECTIONS

In order to make a map, a 3D shape has to be projected onto a flat surface. Most maps and charts use one of the variants of the **Mercator** projection. The advantage of this map projection is that it preserves angles. A constant course heading is shown as a straight line. To keep the proportions needed to achieve this, minutes of latitude have to be drawn proportionally bigger as we move towards the poles. This is only really obvious on charts that cover large areas. The way we cope with this is to measure distances on the latitude scale as close to the latitude of the location we are measuring as possible.

With problems towards the poles in the Mercator projection, map makers turn to one or other form of polar projection, which you may encounter when planning trips within the high arctic.

For ocean crossing voyages, large scale **gnomonic** projection charts are used (find out more about this if you plan such a voyage!) You may encounter the gnomonic projection on some detailed charts of harbours but at such scales the differences between projections are negligible for the kayaker.

Symbols & abbreviations

Maps and charts aimed at leisure users usually have a key (or legend) which show the symbols and abbreviations used.

Booklets describing in detail all the symbols used on nautical charts are available. Admiralty charts are covered by the publication 'Symbols and Abbreviations used on Admiralty Charts 5011'. US charts are covered by the pamphlet 'Chart No 1, Nautical Chart Symbols and Abbreviations'. Any yacht chandlers will have these and publications listing all the charts that these agencies produce.

Chart No 1 (above right) is now out of print and available as a download only.

For this section it is vital that you constantly refer to the chart on page 24.

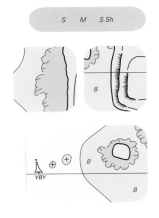

Weekly 'Notices to Mariners' appear on the Hydrographic Office website and should be used to update your chart. For example a light may change or a buoy may be moved.

Commonly used chart symbols and abbreviations

Blood and Sludge Bay is marked with the abbreviation S. This means that the bottom consists of sand. Port Gunge, however, is marked with an M which stands for mud so, although a useful escape route, Port Gunge is not a desirable landing place. Port Epic has the abbreviation S Sh, sand and shells, nice place for a picnic.

The shore between Blood and Sludge Bay and Port Gunge is marked by a symbol that indicates a rocky foreshore, whereas between Port Gunge and Port Epic the symbols indicate cliffs.

Port Gunge is to the south of a rock islet that is always uncovered. The two crosses further out to sea represent rocks which are always (but at low water only just) covered by water. These represent a danger to shipping, though not normally to kayakers, so they are marked by a buoy which is distinguished by its top mark, in this case two cones pointing inwards and coloured yellow, black, yellow. Buoyage is covered in detail in Chapter 6. For navigational purposes, in a kayak, all we need is to make sure we have identified the right one. Buoys are distinguished from one another by their colour, shape, or top mark. Important ones will also have a name or number painted on them. All this information is on the chart.

These rocks could be a danger (or fun depending on your skill level) if a big swell is running, as the waves may build up and break over the submerged rocks (reef breaks). The point south of Port Epic has a light at its end; the structure on which the light is raised is usually painted white so you can see it in daylight.

The figure ·128 tells us that the hill above Port Epic is 128 metres above sea level, (MHWS).

The rock off Blood and Sludge Bay is coloured green and marked with a drying height. We are told that it is a drying height by the fact that the 4 is underlined. For a detailed explanation of the difference between heights, drying heights and depths study the illustration below. The larger figure indicates metres and the smaller one by its side tenths of metres. So 4_5 indicates a drying height of 4.5 metres. This means it would be covered at high water but, as the tide went out, it would dry out, in this case when the tide was 4.5 metres above chart datum. A mark like an asterisk indicates a small isolated drying rock. The figures offshore tell us the depths below chart datum (the lowest possible tide).

Heights and depths.
Profile of the sea bed with
inset of chart symbols.

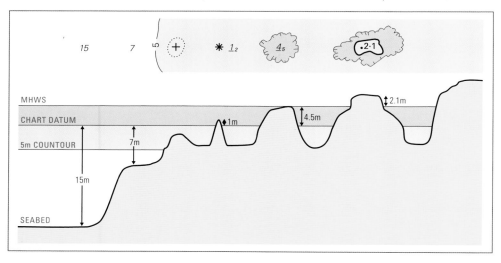

EXERCISES

1 Find on a land map an example of as many of the symbols shown on the key (legend) as you can find.

2 Do the same for a chart that has a key.

5 BASIC NAVIGATION

Many journeys can be undertaken without even the need to draw a line on a chart. All that is needed is some simple planning, after which you can get to your destination by following the coastline and using landmarks, buoys and transits to find your way and keep track of your progress.

Direction

The simplest way to use the map or chart is to orientate it to the ground, revealing where landmarks are in relation to each other and to our position.

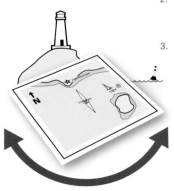

1. Find your current position on the chart.

2. Turn the chart, using your position as the centre of rotation, until an obvious feature on the land is in line with the same feature on the chart (in this case a lighthouse).

3. Facing that feature, you should find that all other features marked on the chart are at the same angle to your position on the chart as they are on the ground.

Once orientated, if a buoy on the chart is 90° right of your position facing the lighthouse, if you look over your right shoulder you will see the buoy.

Distance, speed, time taken

When planning a day's journey, first consider what will be a reasonable distance for your group. The following estimates, which are based on my experience, assume calm or light winds and make no allowance for the help or hindrance of tides.

DISTANCES	SPEEDS
Relative novice **4–6NM**	Relative novice .... **2kn or less**
Average 'weekend' paddler **10–12NM**	Average 'weekend' paddler in general purpose kayak .... **2kn** in sea kayak **3kn**
'Committed' sea paddler **20NM**	
Extreme paddler (on a mission) ...... **40NM*** *anywhere up to 100NM	Fast sea paddler **3.5–4kn**

Time taken

Now, by simply dividing distance by speed, we can work out how long a journey should take.

For example: a journey of 12 nautical miles divided by 3 knots (speed of average sea paddlers) would take four hours.

The problem with this calculation is that it assumes non-stop paddling from A to B. This works fine if you are paddling across a bay from point to point. However, if you are paddling along a stretch of coastline you may wish to add, say, one hour for exploring the more interesting bits, plus one hour for rests, lunch, casting doubts on the leader's navigation and so on. The total time taken might be six hours.

PLANNING A SIMPLE PASSAGE

The following planning is for taking a group of relative novices from Blood and Sludge Bay to Port Epic and return. There are no tidal streams and weather conditions are sunny with gentle onshore winds.

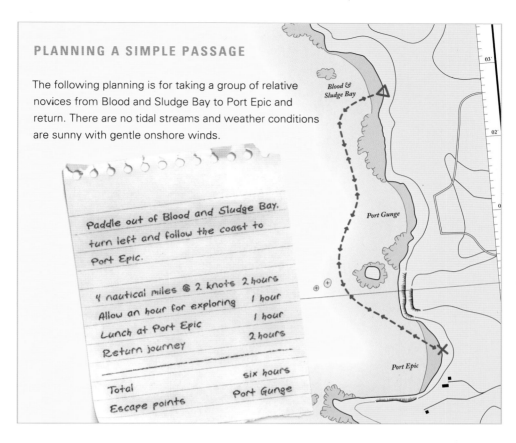

Paddle out of Blood and Sludge Bay.
turn left and follow the coast to
Port Epic.

4 nautical miles @ 2 knots	2 hours
Allow an hour for exploring	1 hour
Lunch at Port Epic	1 hour
Return journey	2 hours
Total	six hours
Escape points	Port Gunge

Keeping track of progress

1 cable = one tenth of a nautical mile or about 200 metres.

If you are following the coastline close inshore, say within a few cables of the shore, progress can be checked by simply noting when you pass prominent features that are marked on the chart.

When paddling further offshore, the passage planning you have done before setting off will allow you to work out your approximate position by working out what distance you have covered in a given time, travelling at a given speed. For instance if you paddle for half an hour at 3 knots you will cover 1.5 nautical miles. This process is known as '**dead reckoning**'.

Dead reckoning

The distance between Bonecrusher Rock and Broken Head is 4.7NM. For those who struggle with mental arithmetic a good solution is to use a 'ready reckoner'. For example, to work out how long it would take to paddle 4.7 nautical miles at 3 knots, go down the left hand column until you get to 4, then move across till you intersect the 3 knot column, this gives you 1 hour 20 minutes. Repeating the procedure for 0.7 of a nautical mile gives you 14 minutes. Add the two together and you have 1 hour 34 minutes.

Ready reckoner for computing speed, distance and time without the arithmetic!

distance (NM)	speed (kn)				
	2	2.5	3	3.5	4
0.1	3min	2min 24s	2min	1min 42s	1min 30s
0.2	6min	4min 48s	4min	3min 24s	3min
0.3	9min	7min 12s	6min	5min 6s	4min 30s
0.4	12min	9min 36s	8min	6min 48s	6min
0.5	15min	12min	10min	8min 30s	7min 30s
0.6	18min	14min 24s	12min	10min 6s	9min
0.7	21min	16min 48s	14min	12min	10min 30s
0.8	24min	19min 12s	16min	13min 42s	12min
0.9	27min	21min 36s	18min	15min 24s	13min 30s
1	30min	24min	20min	17min	15min
2	1hr	48min	40min	34min	30min
3	1hr 30min	1hr 12min	1hr	51min	45min
4	2hr	1hr 36min	1hr 20min	1hr 8min	1hr
5	2hr 30min	2hr	1hr 40min	1hr 26min	1hr 15min

Estimating your speed in a kayak is not an exact science and, as we will discover in later chapters, allowing for tide and wind involves some margin for error. Therefore it is useful to confirm your position from time to time. Using observations to establish your position is known as getting a '**fix**'.

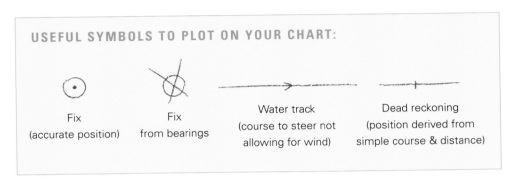

USEFUL SYMBOLS TO PLOT ON YOUR CHART:

Fix
(accurate position)

Fix
from bearings

Water track
(course to steer not
allowing for wind)

Dead reckoning
(position derived from
simple course & distance)

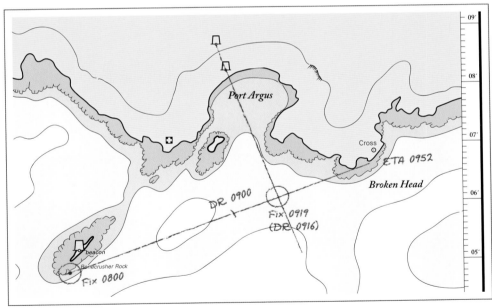

Two simple ways of finding your position – passing
close to a prominent feature and using transits.

Two ways of finding your position are shown on page 33. At 0800 our paddler passes close by Bonecrusher Rock, the simplest way of getting a fix.

Between the rock and Broken Head travelling in a straight line a **transit** can be used to obtain a new fix. A transit is the line between two prominent visible landmarks (in some cases lights or beacons positioned for this purpose). To use a transit to gain a fix, note the time when the two landmarks align, find them on the chart, draw a line between them and then extend that line out to sea. Where the transit crosses your path provides a fix for that time (given in this case that your path is another straight line). The distance between Bonecrusher Rock and the fix provided by the transit is 3.8NM. At 3 knots it should take 1 hour 16 minutes to cover that distance. Leaving at 0800 you could expect to arrive in line with the transit at 0916.

The transit beacons in Port Argus. First to the west of the transit, then inline, finally passing east of the transit. Any two prominent objects can be used as transit markers, as long as one is further away than the other.

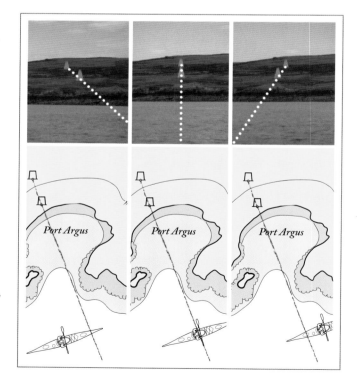

In the example illustrated on page 33 the time taken to reach intersection with the transit is 3 minutes later than calculated by dead reckoning. It may however be unnecessary to recalculate the remaining part of the crossing to Broken Head since the times and distances involved are small.

CALCULATION

If you like mathematics, the dead reckoning calculation is:

$$\frac{Distance\ (NM)}{Speed\ (kn)} = \frac{Time}{(hours)}$$

The distance to where the transit and the course paddled cross is 3.8NM. Given an average paddling speed of 3kn the time taken to reach this point is:

$$\frac{3.8\ NM}{3kn} = 1\ hour\ 16\ min$$

EXERCISES

1 Work out a passage plan for the last simple coastal journey you went on. Compare your workings with the time you actually took.

2 Work out a passage plan for the next simple coastal journey you are going on. When you have completed the journey, compare the time taken with the time predicted. Make a note of how you might adjust your calculations in future.

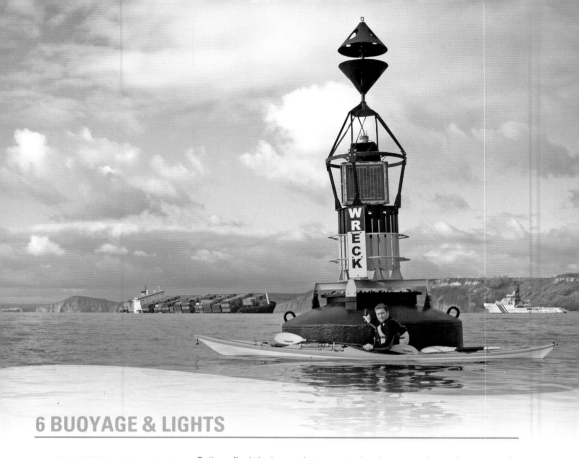

6 BUOYAGE & LIGHTS

The MSC Napoli, wrecked off the Cornish coast in January 2007. Marked by an east cardinal mark.

Sailors find their way into port using buoys and transits to stay in the deep water channel. Kayakers need to understand the basics of buoyage and lights in order to be able to stay out of the way of other craft. In channels, most boats are 'restricted in their ability to manoeuvre' because if they change course they will run aground. So stay outside the deep water channel to avoid being run down. Buoys can also help us fix our position.

Spars or perches

In places, posts are driven into the seabed. These marks serve the same function as buoys. Similar to buoys they are distinguished by colour and a 'topmark'.

Port marker perch.

LATERAL MARKS

Region A: Europe, Australia, New Zealand, parts of Africa and parts of Asia.

R   R
red light
(any rhythm)

G   G
green light
(any rhythm)

DIRECTION OF BUOYAGE

Region B: North, Central and South America, Philippines and Japan.

G   G
green light
(any rhythm)

R   R
red light
(any rhythm)

DIRECTION OF BUOYAGE

CARDINAL MARKS (both regions)

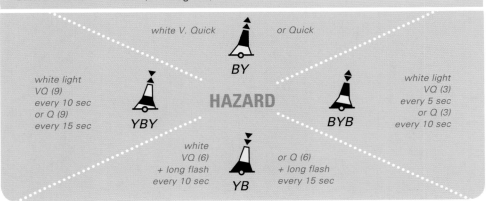

white V. Quick   or Quick

BY

white light
VQ (9)
every 10 sec
or Q (9)
every 15 sec   YBY

HAZARD

BYB   white light
VQ (3)
every 5 sec
or Q (3)
every 10 sec

white
VQ (6)
+ long flash
every 10 sec   YB   or Q (6)
+ long flash
every 15 sec

ISOLATED DANGER MARKS

white light group flashing (2)

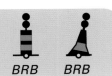

BRB   BRB

SAFE WATER MARKS

white isophase, occulting,
or 1 long flash every 10 sec

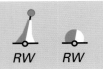

RW   RW

SPECIAL MARK

yellow light (any rhythm)

Y

*International Association of Lighthouse Authorities

Lateral buoys

These are the general principles. Refer to your chart for local exceptions.

These buoys are usually used to mark the deep water channels. The marks are standardized worldwide, in the interests of international shipping – however there is an historical variation in use across the Atlantic, systems A and B.

PORT – *left facing the front of the boat.* **STARBOARD** – *right facing the front of the boat.*

IALA A

Port markers are painted red, shaped like a tin can, and are kept to port as ships make their way up the channel into the harbour.

Channel marker buoys come in many different sizes but they all use the same shapes and topmarks. Here we have an example of a port mark (left) and starboard mark (right).

Where the direction of buoyage is not obviously linked to a harbour it usually corresponds with the direction of the flood tide. The only way to be certain is to look on the chart where it is indicated by the use of the symbol above.

Starboard markers are green, cone shaped and kept to starboard as ships go up the channel. When coming out of the harbour and heading out towards the sea the procedure is reversed; green buoys are kept to the left and red ones are kept to the right.

IALA B

This system is used, notably in North America and Japan, where you will find the buoy's colours (but not shapes) are reversed as for system A. Green cans are kept to the left and red cones to the right as vessels go into harbour.

Cardinal marks

Cardinal marks refer to the 'cardinal' points of the compass; i.e. north, south, east and west. A west cardinal mark means that the clear water is to the west of the mark, and that the mark is to the west of the danger. They are painted a combination of yellow and black bands. The topmarks are easy to remember.

 North – Two black cones both point upwards. North is usually the top of a map.

 South – Two black cones both point downwards. South is usually the bottom of a map.

 East – The cones point away from each other, forming a diamond shape.

 West – The cones point towards each other forming a 'waist'.

Other marks

Fairway or safe water marks

These are 'landfall' buoys to mark the seaward limit of a buoyed channel. Occasionally used to mark the middle of the channel.

Isolated danger marks

These indicate an isolated danger with deep water all around it.

Special marks

Any buoy or spar that is coloured yellow has a special meaning which will need to be looked up on the chart.

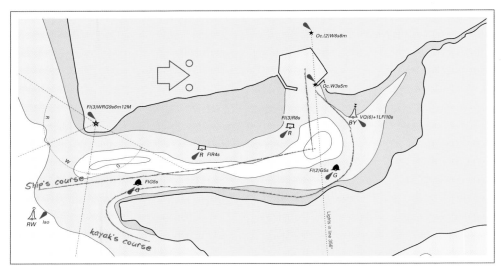

IALA system A in the approaches to a harbour.

Lights

Lights are described on charts using standard abbreviations. Refer to the chart above and I will describe a selection that cover all the types of abbreviation you are likely to come across.

The lighthouse (★) reads:
Fl (3) WRG 9s 6m 12M

9 seconds

Fl means flashing, a flash of light lasts half a second, with an equal length of darkness until the next flash. **(3)** means a group of three (in this case three flashes). **WRG** means white, red and green. This light has all three colours in different sectors. White is the correct angle of approach, (from the sea), red is too far left, green is too far right (for a large vessel). **9s**, nine seconds is the period taken to show one group of flashes. **6m**, six metres is the height of the light above MHWS. **12M**, twelve nautical miles is the distance you could expect to see the light from in good visibility.

The south cardinal buoy (⟁) reads: **VQ(6)+1LFl 10s**

10 seconds

VQ means very quick flash, half as long as a flash, in this case six of them. **LFl** means long flash, twice as long as a flash. **10s**, ten seconds. The period between sequences. If the light's colour is omitted, it is a white light.

The most southerly port mark (⌐R⌐), reads: **Fl R 4s**

This means a single red flash every four seconds.

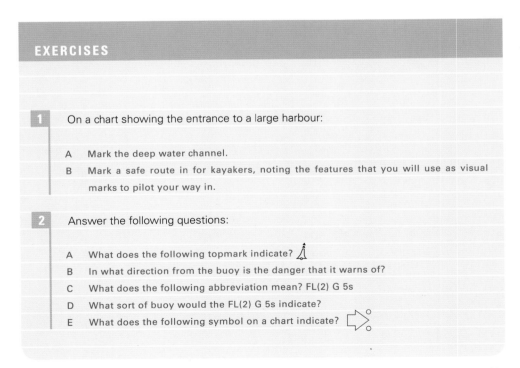

The other port mark (⌐R⌐) reads: **Fl (3) R 8s**

This red can is distinguished by a different group and period.

The pier head light (★) reads: **OC W 3s 5m**

OC means occulting. This is where the light is on most of the time and there is a half second 'flash' of darkness.

The safe water mark (⌀) reads: **Iso**

Iso means that the light and dark periods are of equal length.

EXERCISES

1 On a chart showing the entrance to a large harbour:

A   Mark the deep water channel.

B   Mark a safe route in for kayakers, noting the features that you will use as visual marks to pilot your way in.

2 Answer the following questions:

A   What does the following topmark indicate? ⌀

B   In what direction from the buoy is the danger that it warns of?

C   What does the following abbreviation mean? FL(2) G 5s

D   What sort of buoy would the FL(2) G 5s indicate?

E   What does the following symbol on a chart indicate? ⇨

7 THE COMPASS

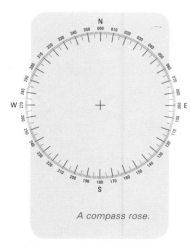

A compass rose.

The compass is a device for finding direction, even when we can't see our destination. The compass needle points to magnetic north, and by measuring an angle from north we can steer a compass course. For example, if our destination is due east of our position, we measure off 90° from north (090°).

True north

All charts and most maps use the North Pole as north, which is known as true north. When we measure off an angle to north on a chart we refer to it as a true bearing. When written we add a capital T. For example a bearing of due south taken off a chart would be written 180°T.

Magnetic north

Compass needles point towards a magnetic north caused by the Earth's magnetic field, which is not in the same direction as true north. When we write a magnetic bearing we add a capital M. For example 180°M, is 180 degrees due south of magnetic North.

Magnetic variation

When we take a bearing from a chart we have to add or subtract a certain number of degrees to allow for the difference between true north and magnetic north before we can use it to steer. This difference is known as magnetic variation (or variation for short).

For a person in Scotland who is facing the North Pole, magnetic north is to the west of true north. Turn the book around so that the writing 'Seward Peninsula' is the right way up and you will see that for a person on the Seward Peninsula, Alaska, who is facing the North Pole, magnetic north is to the east of true north.

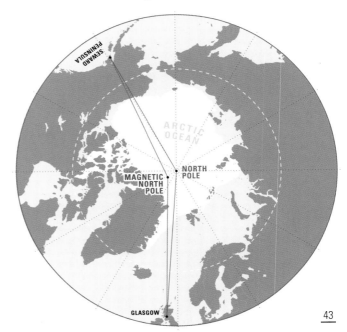

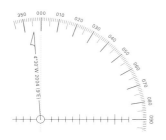

Magnetic variation as appears on an Admralty Leisure Series chart; here it is stated as 4°30' west in 2004 changing approximately 9' east annually.

Finding variation

All maps and charts bear a note of the variation for the area covered. Charts have this information included on the compass rose. A chart that covers a very large area may have several roses, in which case the information is taken from the nearest one. The Earth's magnetic field fluctuates in a predictable manner; to allow for which a small adjustment is made as time passes. This information will be presented something like: Variation 6° west for 2004, changing approximately 6' east annually. For this example variation will be 5° west in the year 2014.

Allowing for variation

In practice when you need to convert a magnetic bearing from your compass to a true bearing you will need to add or subtract the variation. If the variation is west, add it to your magnetic bearing to find the true bearing. If the variation is east, subtract it. A good way to remember this is to use the old seafarer's rhyme:

ERROR WEST, COMPASS BEST. ERROR EAST, COMPASS LEAST

Using a Portland Plotter and marking the correct variation for the area you are navigating in we can convert the bearing instantly by reading off the bearing at the pencil mark (10°W).

Example; converting from true to magnetic

This is what to do if you wish to take a bearing off the chart and convert it so that it is corrected for use with the compass. If you live somewhere where the compass needle points to the west of true north you have to add the variation. For example if variation is 10° west you would make the following allowance:

Course from chart	135°T
Variation	10°W
Course to steer	145°m

If you live where the compass needle points to the east of true north you have to subtract variation. If variation is 10° east:

Remember when writing down a magnetic bearing to put an 'M' after it so that we know that it has already been converted.

Course from chart	135°T
Variation	10°E
Course to steer	125°M

Example; converting from magnetic to true

This is what to do if you wish to take a bearing with a compass and convert it so that it is corrected for use on the chart.

In the following example variation is 15° west:

Compass bearing	210°M
Variation	15°W
Bearing on chart	195°T

In the following example variation is 15° east:

Bearing from compass	210°M
Variation	15°E
Bearing on chart	225°T

TECHNICAL STUFF!

Strictly speaking, there are three types of north: **True north** (T), taken off a chart. **Magnetic north** (M), requiring allowance for variation. **Compass north** (C), requiring allowance for deviation.

Deviation is the pull exerted on the compass needle by large lumps of metal on a boat, such as its engine. This is irrelevant to sea kayakers, as long as ferrous metal (iron and steel) objects are not packed right next to the compass! So forget it!

No chart work approach

In practice, on journeys that involve following a coastline, the compass will probably only be used in fog. Even then it needn't involve any chart work. In the unlikely event that the fog engulfs you before you manage to read the bearing off the compass, a very crude use of the compass will usually do. Refer back to page 33 and imagine that you are overtaken by a sudden fog somewhere between Bonecrusher Rock and Broken Head. No matter where you are on that course, if you steer due north, (000°T), you will come back in sight of land.

If you simply point your kayak towards Broken Head, you can read the bearing off the compass and keep paddling on that bearing.

Types of compass

Hillwalking compasses are cheap and unlikely to be damaged or stolen. However you have to keep looking down in order to read them and over a long distance this can cause discomfort or even seasickness.

Hillwalking compass

If the nature of the coastline is such that a compass is rarely needed, a handheld one, as used by mountaineers and hikers, can be carried in a buoyancy aid pocket. This type of compass doubles as a protractor for chart work and when wedged under the deck elastics or taped to the deck is adequate for steering a course over a short distance.

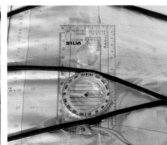

To take a bearing for a course to steer with a pocket compass:

1.   Sight along the travel line of the compass,

2.   Turn the bezel until the arrow on the bezel lines up with the needle
      with the arrow pointing to the red end of the needle.

3.   Fix the compass to the deck so that the 'direction of travel' line is
      pointing forward.

4.   Turn your kayak till the needle points in the same direction as the
      arrow in he bezel. Keep adjusting course so that the needle and
      the arrow keep pointing in the same direction.

Deck mounted compass

When paddling in a location where there are long open crossings
or frequent fog, a proper deck mounted 'steering' compass is
a must. These compasses are mounted well forward, allowing
paddlers to look where they are going as well as at the compass.

To take a bearing for a course to steer, point your kayak in the
direction required, read off the bearing, and then keep adjusting
your course so that the bearing remains the same.

DON'T STARE AT THE COMPASS

Steering is much easier if you set up the course using the compass and then use other
indicators to stay on course, checking them against the compass every few minutes. Use
distant features or clouds, but keep changing them when you check against the compass
(especially clouds!) Wind, swell and wave direction are other clues.

SWINGING THE COMPASS

In practice, when steering a compass course in any sea state other than flat calm, you will
not be able to keep the course steady. The waves will cause the boat to steer first to one
side and then to the other by a few degrees. The trick is to try and ensure that the swing
is as even as possible so that the errors cancel each other out.

Chart work

'Laying-off' – working out a bearing by drawing it on a chart.

The best way to start is by drawing a straight line on the chart between where we are and where we want to go. Yachtsmen use a soft pencil but we need to laminate our maps with plastic in order to use them at sea, so a permanent overhead projector marker is best for passage planning (it won't get accidentally rubbed off and can be removed later using alcohol). For **laying-off** a course whilst afloat a Chinagraph pencil is best.

To find out what angle from north a given point on a map is you need some form of protractor. For working things out before you set off a 'Breton' or 'Portland Plotter' is ideal (opposite page). Unfortunately they are too large to be conveniently used on the front deck of a sea kayak and a large Silva Expedition 4, or similar mountaineering compass can be used as a plotter/protractor.

Laying-off a bearing

A Portland Plotter is used to lay-off a course from a position one cable (200 metres), west of the buoy off Port Gunge, to the southern end of Blood and Sludge Bay.

1. Draw a line between your position and the destination, (Blood and Sludge Bay).

2. Lay the edge of the plotter, or one of the parallel lines that run along its length, against the course line, with the large triangle pointing in the direction of travel.

3. Turn the circular protractor, until the lines that form a grid in its centre are lined up with one of the latitude or longitude lines that cross the chart, and the two small triangles are pointed at the top of the chart (north).

4. Read the bearing off the scale where it is marked zero, in this case 024°T.

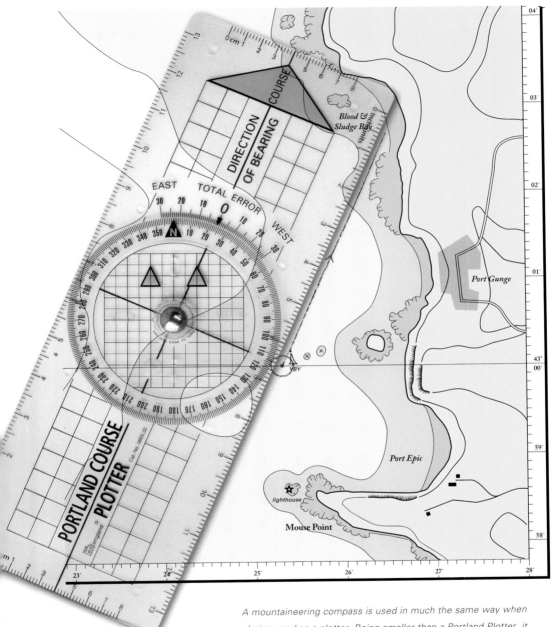

A mountaineering compass is used in much the same way when being used as a plotter. Being smaller than a Portland Plotter, it will probably be necessary to draw on your course first with a ruler before measuring the angle. And you'll need to ignore the needle!

Steering 270°M.

To steer a course taken from a chart

Lay-off the bearing on a chart or map, this gives you a true bearing (T). Adjust for variation. This turns it into a magnetic bearing (M) which is your 'course to steer'. With a deck mounted compass, simply turn your kayak until the figures on the compass match the course to steer.

Steering 270°M.

To steer a course with a hillwalking compass:

1. Turn the bezel so that the desired course is indicated.

2. Fix the compass to the deck so that the 'direction of travel' line is pointing down the centre line of the kayak.

3. Alter course until the red needle points in the same direction as the bezel arrow.

EXERCISES

1 Use your plotter of choice to find the following true bearings on page 49:

A   From the buoy to the lighthouse.
B   From the buoy to the centre of the reef off Blood & Sludge Bay.
C   From the buoy to the northernmost building at Port Epic.

2 If a bearing was 235°T, what would be the magnetic bearing if the variation was:

A   5°W   B   7°E

3 If a bearing was 235°M, what would be the true bearing if the variation was:

A   9°W   B   3°E

4 Practice steering a compass course on your next trip. There is a knack to it that is best learnt before you need it for real.

8 POSITION

By taking bearings of prominent objects on the land that are marked on the chart, we can get a fix even where there are no transits available. The nearer the angle between the two bearings is to 90°, the more accurate the resulting fix will be. (Fix A below.) We can of course get a fix by combining a transit and a bearing (Fix B below.)

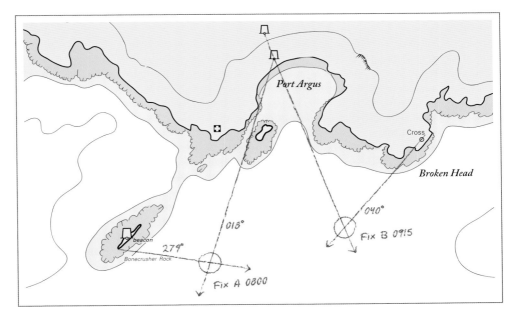

If you need to let someone know your position, you can give it in one of two forms: a map reference such as latitude and longitude, or as a bearing and distance.

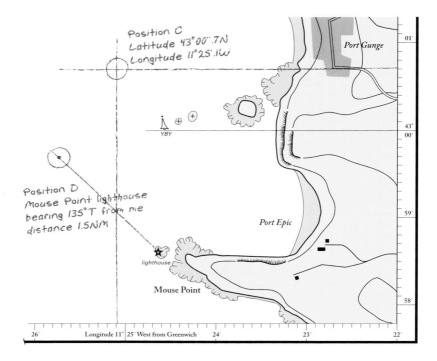

Position C
Latitude 43°00".7N
Longitude 11°25'.1W

Port Gunge

01'

YBY

43°
00'

Position D
Mouse Point lighthouse
bearing 135°T from me
distance 1.5NM

59'

Port Epic

lighthouse

58'

Mouse Point

26'   Longitude 11° 25' West from Greenwich   24'   23'   22'

Latitude & longitude

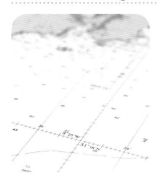

By drawing a line **horizontally** across the chart to where it intersects the latitude scale you can read off the latitude part of your position. You then draw a line **vertically** until it intersects the longitude scale and read off the longitude. In the example above, Position A is given as latitude 43°00'.7 N (north) and longitude 11°25'.1 W (west).

With the popularity of GPS (Global Positioning System) recent nautical charts have a grid laid over their surface at 1' intervals. This makes it much quicker and easier to plot latitude and longitude.

Latitude and longitude.

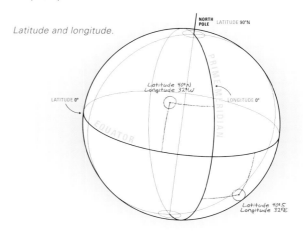

Bearing & distance

The other way is to give your bearing and distance off a prominent landmark. In the example below, Position D is 1.5 NM to the north-west of Mouse Point, which means that if a kayaker takes a bearing of the point, and corrects to allow for variation, the result will be a bearing of 135°T because the point is to the south-east of the kayaker. Conversely, if someone on the shore at Mouse Point were to take a bearing of the kayaker, they would get a bearing of 315°T. It is therefore possible to give your bearing and distance in two ways:

1. "My position is, bearing from Shipwreck Point 315°T, distance 1.5 nautical miles."

2. "My position is, Shipwreck Point bearing from me 135°T, distance 1.5 nautical miles."

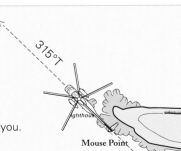

315°T

Lighthouse

Mouse Point

1 Using the chart on page 52, give the position of the west cardinal buoy as a latitude and longitude.

2 Using the chart on page 52, give the position of the west cardinal buoy as a bearing and distance from the lighthouse in the format you would use if reporting your position to the emergency services.

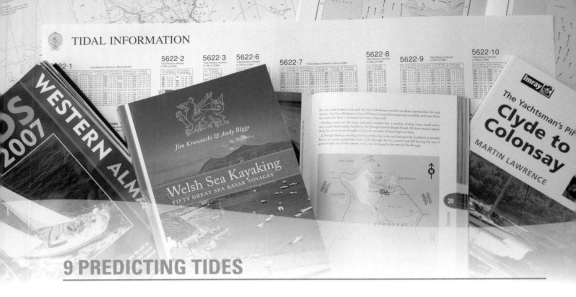

9 PREDICTING TIDES

There are five main sources of tidal stream information:

- Nautical charts.

- Tidal stream atlases.

- Admiralty or yachting pilots.

- Sea kayaking guides.

- Nautical almanacs.

Nautical almanacs gather together a lot of the information found in a variety of other sources.

Nautical charts give useful information, but only in specific places where large ships most need it. Tidal stream atlases are great when you are well out to sea but are not very helpful close inshore. Pilot books and sea kayaking guides are probably the most useful as they have the most detailed information close inshore.

In order to make use of any of these you need to know the time of HW and whether it is a spring or neap tide. For this you will need a tide table. Predicting tides by knowing what time HW was the day before and what phase of the moon it is works very well but is not practical if you live away from the sea, or are going to drive to somewhere different.

Tide tables

A tide table sets out the date, time and height of high water and low water. In Britain, the time is usually given as Greenwich Mean Time (GMT). During British Summer Time (BST) from the 30th of March to the 26th of October, remember to add 1 hour to convert from GMT to BST. Wherever in the world you are, it is important to check whether you need to make an allowance for local time. Heights are measured above chart datum.

Liverpool tide tables for the month of August.

| | High Water | | | | | | Low Water | | | | | |
| | am | | | pm | | | am | | | pm | | |
Date	Time	M	Ft	Time	M	Ft	Time	M	Ft	Time	M	Ft
1 Mon	0530	7.2	23.6	1810	7.1	23.3				1206	3.2	10.5
2 Tue	0650	7.1	23.3	1931	7.3	24.0	0055	3.4	11.2	13.25	3.2	10.5
3 Wed	0804	7.4	24.3	2034	7.7	25.3	0212	3.1	10.2	1435	2.9	9.5
4 Thu	0900	7.8	25.6	2125	8.2	26.9	0314	2.6	8.5	1537	2.5	8.2
5 Fri	0948	8.3	27.2	2207	8.7	28.5	0406	2.1	6.9	1619	2.0	6.6
6 Sat	1028	8.7	28.5	2247	9.1	21.9	0452	1.7	5.6	1704	1.6	5.2
7 Sun	1106	9.1	29.9	2325	9.4	30.8	0536	1.3	4.3	1744	1.3	4.3
8 Mon	1146	9.3	30.5				0618	0.9	3.0	1826	1.0	3.3
9 Tue	0003	9.6	31.5	1225	9.5	31.2	0657	0.7	2.3	1906	0.9	3.0
10 Wed	0042	9.7	31.8	1303	9.5	31.2	0737	0.6	2.0	1945	0.9	3.0
11 Thu	0120	9.7	31.8	1344	9.3	30.5	0816	0.8	2.6	2024	1.1	3.6
12 Fri	0200	9.5	31.2	1426	9.1	21.9	0854	1.1	3.6	2102	1.4	4.6
13 Sat	0244	9.1	29.9	1511	8.7	28.5	0935	1.4	4.6	2150	1.8	5.9
14 Sun	0335	8.7	28.5	1610	8.3	27.2	1023	2.0	6.6	2245	2.2	7.2
15 Mon	0438	8.2	26.9	1719	7.9	25.9	1127	2.4	7.9			
16 Tue	0559	7.8	25.6	1842	7.9	25.9	0002	2.6	8.5	1252	2.6	8.5
17 Wed	0726	7.8	25.6	2001	8.3	27.2	0133	2.5	8.2	1416	2.4	7.9
18 Thu	0842	8.2	26.9	2105	8.7	28.5	0253	2.1	6.9	15.26	2.0	6.6
19 Fri	0941	8.6	28.2	2201	9.1	21.9	0401	1.6	5.2	1625	1.5	4.9
20 Sat	1031	9.0	29.5	2247	9.5	31.2	0457	1.1	3.6	1714	1.1	3.9
21 Sun	1111	9.2	30.2	2326	9.7	31.8	0541	0.8	2.6	1754	0.8	3.3
22 Mon	1151	9.3	30.5				0620	0.7	2.3	1831	0.7	3.3
23 Tue	0005	9.7	31.8	11.25	9.3	30.5	0656	0.8	2.6	1903	1.0	3.3
24 Wed	0039	9.6	31.5	1256	9.1	29.9	0728	10.	3.3	1937	1.2	3.9
25 Thu	0112	9.4	30.8	1326	8.9	29.2	0758	1.2	3.9	2007	1.6	5.2
26 Fri	0143	9.0	29.5	1359	8.6	28.2	0826	1.6	5.2	2036	2.0	6.6
27 Sat	0219	8.7	28.5	1433	8.3	27.2	0853	2.0	6.6	2106	2.4	7.9
28 Sun	0255	8.2	26.9	1511	7.8	25.6	0926	2.5	8.2	2146	2.9	9.5
29 Mon	0336	7.7	25.3	1601	7.4	24.3	1005	3.0	9.8	2241	3.3	10.8
30 Tue	0435	7.2	23.6	1712	7.0	23.0	1106	3.4	11.2			
31 Wed	0556	6.9	22.6	1841	7.1	23.3	0000	3.5	11.5	1233	3.6	11.8

When using real tide tables make sure they are the current year!

TOP TIP

Yachtsmen buy expensive, bulky almanacs, which contain tide tables. This means that they buy a new one every year. Get your hands on an old one and you can cut out and laminate useful items such as the tidal stream atlases. These don't change from year to year and all you need is a set of your local tide tables; a bargain!

If you look at page 56 you will see a set of Liverpool tide tables for the month of August. Tide tables are available for 'standard ports', for example in Britain you would look up Dover for most of the South Coast, Liverpool for the Irish Sea, and Ullapool for the north-west coast of Scotland. The left-hand side of the tide table gives us a.m. and p.m. high water times and heights.

By simply working your way down the height columns you can find the highest HW (springs) and the lowest HW (neaps). In the illustration they are circled. If we assume we wish to paddle on Wednesday 10th August (underlined), we can work out that HW Liverpool is at 1303 GMT, or 1403 BST (local time), and that it will be spring tides.

Mean springs and neaps

The tables also provide us with the information that the mean spring range is 8.4m and the mean neap range 4.5m.

On the 10th August, HW is 9.5m and the following LW is 0.9m. Subtracting the LW from the HW gives a range of 8.6m. This is slightly higher than the mean spring range.

Secondary ports

To find out the time of local high water at any point between the standard ports – look up the nearest secondary port. For example, the adjustments for HW at Holyhead is –0048. This means that if HW at Liverpool is 1403, HW at Holyhead is 1315.

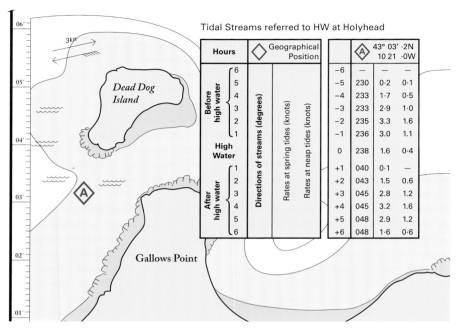

Tidal Streams referred to HW at Holyhead

Hours		◇ Geographical Position	Directions of streams (degrees)	Rates at spring tides (knots)	Rates at neap tides (knots)		◇ A	43° 03′ ·2N 10 21 ·0W	
Before high water	6					−6	—	—	—
	5					−5	230	0·2	0·1
	4					−4	233	1·7	0·5
	3					−3	233	2·9	1·0
	2					−2	235	3·3	1·6
	1					−1	236	3·0	1·1
High Water						0	238	1·6	0·4
After high water	1					+1	040	0·1	—
	2					+2	043	1·5	0·6
	3					+3	045	2·8	1·2
	4					+4	045	3·2	1·6
	5					+5	048	2·9	1·2
	6					+6	048	1·6	0·6

Tidal information on nautical charts.

Tidal streams on charts

MEAN

To be precise, when I say that tidal information refers to springs or neaps, I mean it refers to the average or 'mean' springs or neaps. So if mean springs is given as 6 metres and the rate indicated is 3 knots, and the tidal range on that day is 6.6 metres, we can expect a rate of a little more than 3 knots on this exceptional tide (see page 60, Interpolation).

In most coastal paddling situations, the tide is either with you or against you. It is like being on a conveyor belt. If you do nothing you are carried in whatever direction the conveyor belt is moving. If you paddle against the flow, it takes a long time and a lot of hard work, so it pays to know when the belt and the tidal stream are going your way.

Tidal diamonds

At strategic places for shipping (which are rarely of use to kayakers), you find a diamond shape with a letter. A table, usually found at the edge of the chart, gives you an hourly set (direction) and rate (speed) for the stream at this point. In the illustration you will see that three hours before HW (−3), the set is 233°T and the rate is 2.9 knots on springs, and 1.0 knots on neaps.

Arrows

Arrows are usually in pairs; the one with feathers denotes the flood tide, the other the ebb. Sometimes they have no indication of the rate, other times they will. On the chart opposite there is only one figure; it refers to the maximum spring rate. If there were two figures, the lower would refer to the maximum neap rate (in knots).

Tide races and overfalls

The chart symbol denotes that you may find overfalls at the location, given suitable tidal and weather conditions.

Overfalls (∿∿∿) are what river paddlers would call standing waves. These can become very confused if a swell is running through them. Overfalls can be expected wherever a reasonably strong tidal stream is 'squeezed', going from deep water over a shallow bank or reef, through the gap between an island and the mainland (as on our chart on the south-east side of the sound between Dead Dog Island and the mainland), or around a head-land. As water is squeezed past these obstructions it speeds up forming a tide race. When the fast flowing water hits slower deep water the resulting friction can cause overfalls.

If you are after excitement and are sure you can handle it, you will want to be there when the tide runs fastest, usually three hours after it last turned. On the other hand, you may wish to sneak past when the tide is on the turn, around slack water, and there is little if any horizontal movement.

Some overfalls only appear on the flood and not on the ebb, or vice versa. Some only appear when the wind blows in the op-posite direction to the tidal stream, 'wind over tide'. Wind over tide will always ensure that the overfalls are bigger than usual. A rough sea state can increase the size of the waves still further and will certainly make them more confused. For details you should always consult the pilot.

Tidal stream atlases

These booklets show you the **set** (direction) and **rate** (speed) of the tidal stream at hourly intervals. The figure overleaf shows the page of a tidal stream atlas for three hours after high water at Dover (+3).

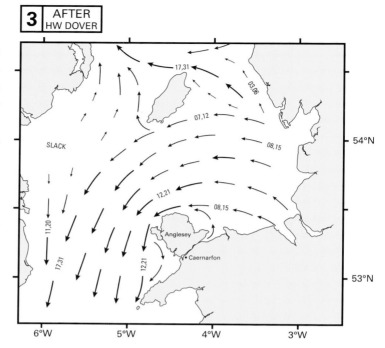

Tidal stream atlas of the NW section of the Irish Sea. Each page of the atlas shows each hour before and after high water. In Britain the pages refer to HW Dover. Wherever in the world you are, if you buy a tidal stream atlas, be sure to also buy a set of the tide tables for the standard port they refer to.

DETAIL

Note the limitations of such atlases – close inshore to the NW coast of Anglesey the pilot tells us that the spring rate at this stage is 4.5 knots. Out to sea it is only 2.1 knots.

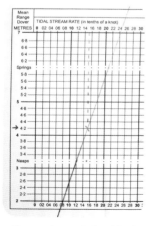

Above ~ interpolating tides in the front of your tidal atlas.

The arrows show the direction and strength of the tidal stream, the bigger the arrow the faster the flow. The figures refer to the speed of the tidal stream. For example – 12,21 – the first figure is the neap speed of the tidal stream in tenths of a knot, and the second figure is the spring speed. So if HW Dover is 0600 hours and we want to know what the tidal streams are doing at 0900, we turn to the page marked three hours after HW Dover. In the position we expect to be in (off the north coast of Anglesey), we see an arrow pointing SW. This gives us our **set** (direction). The figures 12,21 tell us that the neap rate will be 1.2 knots and the spring rate will be 2.1 knots.

Interpolation

Tidal stream atlases provide you with an easy to use graph to help you interpolate tidal stream rates. After finding the figures in the location and on the time in question (e.g. 12,21) and then:

- Plot the spring rate and the neap rate on the appropriate line.

- Draw a line between them.

- Read off the figure where the line crosses the tidal range at Dover on the day in question (in this example 1.5kn).

BEWARE

In many locations tidal stream atlases are of limited use to canoeists; they refer to deep water and commercial shipping channels and do not usually give much indication of what is happening close to land. They are however very useful on open crossings and they do give you an overall picture of what is happening.

An illustration of this is Orkney, where tidal streams are strong everywhere and commercial shipping abundant. Therefore the tidal stream atlas is very useful. In contrast in neighbouring Shetland, where tidal streams are generally weak, pilots are far more useful.

Pilot books

There are other pilots, some produced by other national hydrographers and some produced by individual yachtsmen.

For kayakers, the most useful source of tidal information is often the Admiralty Pilot. This series of books covers the whole world in useful stretches of coast. Each chapter will begin with a description of the coastline which you can either read, while referring to a chart, or ignore and go straight to the section on 'Tidal Streams'.

The pilot might read, "Along the coast off Hangman's Bay, the west-going stream begins −0455 HW Holyhead. The east-going stream begins +0110 HW Holyhead. Streams in both directions achieve a maximum spring rate of 2.1 knots". Note that in most places the tide goes in one direction with the flood and the opposite way with the ebb, here W-going equates roughly to flood tide, and E-going to ebb tide. There are however many exceptions; times can differ by hours rather than minutes, so the pilot always refers to direction rather than ebb and flood.

The time at which the tidal set changes does not necessarily correspond to the times of HW and LW! Using the information from the pilot:

10th of August

HW Liverpool	1303 (GMT)	Allow for British
Add one hour for local time	+0100	Summer Time.
	1403 (BST)	

HW Liverpool	1403	Convert to HW
Subtract 48 mins	−0048	Holyhead.
HW Holyhead	1315	

HW Holyhead	1315	Find out when
Subtract 4 hours 55 mins	−0455	West-going stream
West-going stream begins	0820 (early start)	begins (slack water).

HW Holyhead	1315	Find out when
Add 1 hour 10 mins	+0110	East-going stream
East-going stream begins	1425	begins (slack water).

In the example quoted, the tide flows north for 6 hours 5 minutes. If you are planning a three hour paddle west, you do not need to start at 0820. Three hours before the tide turns against you will do (1125). Allowing for delays 1100 would be better. Often this is all you need to know on a straightforward coastal trip. Sometimes, however, you need to work out your speed fairly accurately.

The owner of the chart has added tidal information. The information from the pilot (red ink) is written with a permanent marker. The information from the tide tables is only relevant to 10th August and is written in (black) Chinagraph pencil.

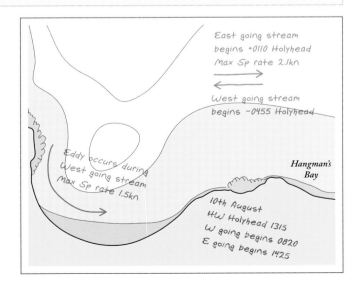

East going stream begins +0110 Holyhead Max Sp rate 2.1kn

West going stream begins −0455 Holyhead

Eddy occurs during West going stream Max Sp rate 1.5kn

Hangman's Bay

10th August
HW Holyhead 1315
W going begins 0820
E going begins 1425

Eddies

The term 'eddy' when used in a pilot refers to a counter current which may be quite strong (not just a patch of slack water). Any counter current strong enough to be mentioned in the pilot cannot be ignored by kayakers.

Eddies are useful when making your way against the tide but a hindrance when going with it. Eddies close inshore are often unmentioned by our sources of tidal stream information and may only be spotted by observation.

Calculating the speed of tidal streams

Out on the open sea the tide turns in an ellipse. Towards slack water the tidal stream changes direction gradually and slows right down but never actually stops altogether.

From the brief information in the pilot we extrapolate rates using the '**50/90 Rule**'. This rule of thumb is based on the fact that most tidal streams increase and decrease at a regular rate.

Where the coastline is complex it is likely that the tide doesn't conform to a normal tidal curve. In this case you will need to read the pilot very carefully for further explanation.

In coastal waters, when the tide turns, there is a period of very little tidal movement which is known as '**slack water**'. These periods do not always coincide with HW and LW. Imagine you are sitting in your kayak at slack water. As the tide turns, the tidal stream begins to flow, slowly at first but gradually becoming more powerful until after three hours the tidal stream reaches its maximum rate of flow. Then, the exact opposite happens, the tide is still moving in the same direction but is gradually slowing down until after about another three hours it goes slack before it turns and runs in the other direction.

The 50/90 Rule

The first stage is to work out what the maximum rate is, given neaps, springs or somewhere in between. Going back to our quote from the pilot, the maximum spring rate is 2.1 knots, the neap rate (unspecified) can be assumed to be about half that of the spring rate. If the tides were neaps, the maximum rate would be estimated at one knot. If they were halfway between neaps and springs the maximum rate would be estimated at 1.5 knots.

hours before/ after slack	0	1	2	3	4	5	6
% of max rate	0% (slack)	50%	90%	100% (max)	90%	50%	0% (slack)
Time	0825	0925	1025	1125	1225	1325	1425
Speed (kn)	0	1.0	1.8	2.1	1.8	1.0	0

On the 10th August we know it is a spring tide; so our maximum rate is 2.1 knots. One hour after the tide turns, the tidal stream is moving at 50% of its maximum rate (one knot). Two hours after the tide turns the stream is running at 90% of its maximum rate. Three hours after slack water the tide is flowing at its maximum rate. After four hours it has decreased in flow to 90% of its maximum rate, after five hours it has slowed to 50% of its maximum rate and after six hours it reaches slack water just before it turns and does the same thing in the opposite direction.

PREDICTING THE HEIGHT OF THE TIDE

The **Rule of Twelfths** is concerned with the height of the tide, not with the speed of tidal streams. Paddlers rarely need to know exactly how deep the water is going to be.

The Rule of Twelfths follows the pattern: 1 2 3 3 2 1. From low to high water, this means that in the first hour after low water the tide rises by one twelfth of its range. In the second by two twelfths, in the third by three twelfths, in the fourth by three twelfths, in the fifth by two twelfths and in the sixth by one twelfth. Between high and low water the tide falls in the same ratios.

Assuming that LW on a given day is 1.0 metres at 0800 and the following HW is 9.4 metres, the tidal range is 8.4 metres. A channel we want to paddle has a drying height of 3 metres (marked on the chart as 3).

One twelfth of the tidal range is 0.7m. Added to the height of low water (1.0 metres above chart datum) gives a height of 1.7m after the first hour. In the second hour the tide rises another two twelfths (1.4m) of its range to 3.1m above chart datum. So we could paddle through the channel at 1000 hours and expect to have 0.1 metres of water under our hulls.

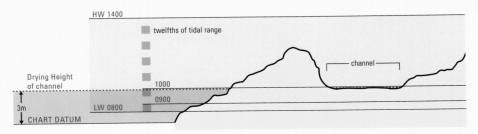

The Rule of Twelfths works on the assumption that the tides are 'normal' (they would, if plotted on a graph, describe a bell-shaped curve). If they are not, the pilot will describe the anomaly in detail. If a tidal diamond or tidal stream atlas cannot be used, the only option is to read the pilot carefully and make diagrams to ensure clarity. Anomalous tides usually occur where water is forced in and out of narrow channels and inlets. Multiple narrow entrances to a body of water complicate matters even further.

Sea kayaking guides

Guides aimed specifically at kayakers have become increasingly available. Their advantage is that they are tailored to our needs and save us having to trawl through a number of sources. The disadvantage is that they don't cover all areas so it is a good idea to be practiced in using all available sources.

Eyeball MK1

This is the most important source of tidal information for sea kayakers. You need to develop your observation skills so that if the tide turns early or late because of weather conditions, or you made a mistake in your calculations, you will spot what is going on.

Even in a weak flow, an anchored buoy will tip in the direction of flow.

In some areas tides are relatively weak and thus poorly reported. However they are still strong enough to give kayakers a hard time and in narrow shallow sounds where yachts and ships don't go they may be locally strong. In these places the 'eyeball mark one' will be your only source of information.

1. The way water surges around a buoy is an obvious clue.

2. Anchored or moored boats will point bows towards the wind or the tide, whichever is strongest. This doesn't apply in narrow places where they moor the boats bow and stern (front and back).

3. The texture and colour of the surface of the sea is affected by the wind and tide. A change in texture may indicate an eddy.

EXERCISES

1 Using tidal diamond A on page 58, what rate would you expect half way between springs and neaps 3 hours after high water Holyhead?

2 What is the spring rate indicated to the east of Anglesey on page 60?

3 If HW Holyhead is 0800 and the S-going stream begins +0120 Holyhead, what time does the S-going stream begin?

4 If the maximum spring rate is 4.2 knots, what is the likely maximum neap rate?

5 If the maximum rate is 5 knots, using the 50/90 Rule, what is the likely rate 1 hour after slack water?

6 Using the example at the foot of page 64:

A   What is the height of water above chart datum after 3 hours?

B   How much water would cover the channel?

10 ALLOWING FOR WIND & TIDE

Under the effects of wind and tide, simple dead reckoning will not give us a usefully accurate position. After making allowances for them, the charted position we come up with is known as an **estimated position**. Indicated by a triangle with a dot at its centre.

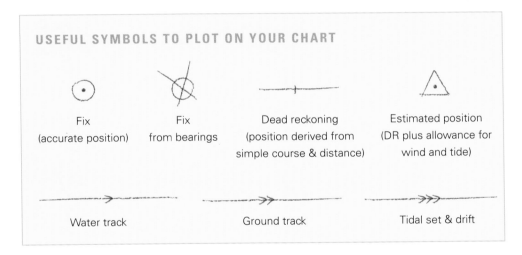

USEFUL SYMBOLS TO PLOT ON YOUR CHART

Fix
(accurate position)

Fix
from bearings

Dead reckoning
(position derived from
simple course & distance)

Estimated position
(DR plus allowance for
wind and tide)

Water track

Ground track

Tidal set & drift

Allowing for tide

When following a coastline, the tide is usually flowing with you or against you. In these situations, the most important thing is to time your journey so as to be helped rather than hindered. To estimate your progress, time elapsed and the speed of the tidal stream must be converted to distance.

BOAT SPEED

The speed at which you move over the water. For example, if you are paddling at 3 knots that is your boat speed.

GROUND SPEED

The speed at which you are moving over the surface of the earth. For example, if you are paddling at 3 knots and a following tidal stream is pushing you along at 2 knots, your ground speed will be 5 knots.

Using tidal diamonds, an atlas or the **50/90 Rule** we work out that at 0925 the tidal stream is running due east at 1 knot. At 1025 it is running at 1.8 knots. If we drifted along with the tide for that period of one hour, how far east would the tidal stream take us?

We have to interpolate the figures (split the difference), and the answer is 1.4 nautical miles. This means that if we add the help we are going to receive from the tide (1.4NM) to our estimate of our distance paddled (one hour at 3 knots = 3NM), we will cover 4.4 nautical miles between 0925 and 1025 hours.

Allowing for a helpful tidal stream.

RULE OF THIRDS

Many people use the rule of thirds to **estimate** how far the tide would move them (tidal drift) over a series of one hour periods. It is quick and easy if not always quite as accurate as interpolating figures gathered from tidal diamonds and tidal stream atlases.

hour before/ after slack	1st	2nd	3rd	4th	5th	6th
rate of drift (thirds of max)	1/3	2/3	3/3	3/3	2/3	1/3

Rule of Thirds calcuated for a maximum spring rate of 2.1 knots (given in the pilot).

Period	0825 0925	0925 1025	1025 1125	1125 1225	1225 1325	1325 1425
Drift (NM)	0.7	1.4	2.1	2.1	1.4	0.7

If you have to plot a course that allows for tide (**shape a course**) whilst you are afloat, you will need to ensure that the information is to hand. Work out the figures for the place and time in question and write them on your planning sheet (see Chapter 14 Planning a Trip).

Left: tidal diamond A as shown on chart. Right: figures for 18th August half way between springs and neaps.

Tidal Streams referred to HW at Holyhead

	A 43° 03′ .2N 10 21 .0W		
-6	—	—	—
-5	230	0·2	0·1
-4	233	1·7	0·5
-3	233	2·9	1·0
-2	235	3.3	1.6
-1	236	3.0	1.1
0	238	1.6	0·4
+1	040	0·1	—
+2	043	1.5	0.6
+3	045	2.8	1.2
+4	045	3.2	1.6
+5	048	2.9	1.2
+6	048	1·6	0·6

A 18th August (BST) range 6.7m

1517	—	—
1617	230	0.1
1717	233	1.1
1817	233	1.9
1917	235	2.4
2017	236	2
HW 2117	238	1
2217	040	—
2317	043	1
0017	045	2
0117	045	2.4
0217	048	2
0317	048	1.1

Cross tides

If the tide isn't flowing exactly with or against us, plot two lines:

1. Plot one hour's worth of course steered. In this example you set off at 0800, have travelled on a course of 270° and covered a distance of 3NM. Make a DR mark.

2. From the DR mark, plot the set and drift of the tide over that hour. The pilot tells you that the tidal stream sets SW at a maximum spring rate of 3 knots. It is a neap tide so the maximum rate is assumed to be 1.5 knots. The course is plotted over the second hour after the tide has turned, so using the rule of thirds you work out that in that one hour period you would drift for 1NM. Therefore set = 225°T (SW) and drift = 1NM.

3. Mark the spot with a triangle and this is the EP at 0900.

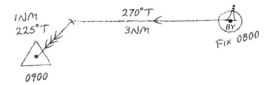

Less than an hour?

Using the same plot as the previous example you wish to know where you would be after 30 minutes (half an hour).

1. Draw a line between the start point fix and your EP. This is the ground track (the path your kayak took rather than the direction it was pointing in), so mark it with two arrowheads.

2. This is also the distance you would have covered over the hour in question. As you wish to know your position after half an hour, make a mark half way along the ground track. This is your EP at 0830.

*In the previous edition of this book I advocated working out the allowance over half hour or 20 minute periods. Although this has always worked well for me I have come to the conclusion that it is **not** the best method, as unless you are very good at mental arithmetic it increases the scope for error.*

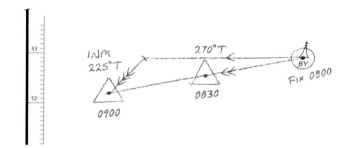

If you need your EP after quarter of an hour, make the mark a quarter of the way along. After 20 minutes, a third of the way along … and so on.

FOR THE MATHEMATICALLY MINDED

1. Draw a line between the start point fix and your EP, mark it with two arrowheads.

2. This is also the distance you would have covered over the hour in question. If you measure it, you'll find that it is 3.8NM long. Speed over the water is 3 knots but your speed over the ground – because the water is also moving over the ground – is 3.8 knots.

3. Work out how much ground you would cover at 3.8kn in 30 minutes = 1.9NM.

4. From the start fix, mark off a distance of 1.9NM along the ground track. Mark the position with a triangle. This is your EP at 0830.

Correcting for tide

FERRY GLIDE

If the tide is running at half our speed we would have to make an allowance of 45° to stay on our desired course. Usually it is not worth ferry gliding in this way if the tide is greater than half your speed as you will have to paddle more against the tide than across it.

An easterly drift of 2.4NM between 0925 and 1025 has been worked out.

Transits

If we can find a transit in line with our desired course, we can simply correct for the tide by adjusting our heading (the direction the kayak is pointing in) to keep the two objects in line, and hence maintain our course.

Shaping a course

In the absence of a transit, if you wish to make a correction that will keep you on your desired course:

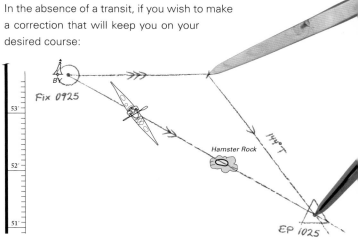

1. Draw a line from your position at 0925, out through and well beyond your intended destination. This is your intended line of travel or ground track so mark it with two arrowheads.

2. Measure the distance between the two positions and estimate how long it would take you to travel between the two using dead reckoning. In this case the distance is less than 3NM, so it would take an hour or less. Therefore, all the calculations are based on a one hour period.

3. From your start point, lay-off a course in the direction in which the tide is travelling, in this case the set is 090°T, and mark off the distance that the tide would cause you to drift, in this case 2.4NM.

4.   Take your dividers, open them to the distance you would paddle in one hour (3NM) and, putting one leg on the end of the tidal drift line, mark the point at which the other leg crosses the ground track. This point is your EP at 1025.

5.   Draw a line between the end of the tidal drift and the EP. This gives you your course to steer (mark it with one arrow), which is 144°T.

For dealing with distances that require more than one hour see Chapter 12 Open Crossings.

Note that in this case the tide has effectively increased your speed over the ground. The target is **roughly** two thirds of the way along the ground track for one hour and it would therefore take you **about** two thirds of an hour (40 minutes) to get there.

FOR THE MATHEMATICALLY MINDED

If you measure the distance along the ground track between the start point and the EP, you'll find that the distance covered over the ground in one hour is 4.8NM. Therefore, as you are travelling at 4.8 knots, with the help of the tide, it will only take you 37 minutes and 30 seconds to cover the 3NM to the island.

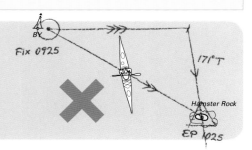

A COMMON MISTAKE

Don't simply draw a line between the tidal set and drift and your destination. This is a very common mistake.

Allowing for wind

Tricky! Tides are very predictable; and we can make calculations to shape a course before setting off. The wind is much more changeable and we can only really make allowances for it once we are afloat. Although we can make a good guesstimate if we have reliable forecasts and stable weather patterns.

Headwinds

Headwinds are hard work and best avoided. How much they will slow you down depends on the type of kayak and on the skill, strength and stamina of the individuals concerned.

Tail winds

On the other hand, a following sea that allows you to surf a good deal of the time could allow you to average 5 knots or more!

Unfortunately all boats have an optimum speed above which they simply won't go. Having the wind behind you will probably only increase your speed by about half a knot more than you can paddle the boat in a flat calm. You will, however, require less effort to paddle at that speed.

Crosswinds

Allowing for crosswinds is very difficult on the open sea. You have to estimate how many degrees you are drifting off course. In yachts the navigator looks at the wake (the disturbed water left by the boat's passage) and estimates how much wake varies from the compass heading. By paddling behind another kayaker we can do the same thing.

Unfortunately if the sea is rough, a kayak's wake is so small that it doesn't leave enough of a track to be effective. Often it comes down to guesstimating your drift based on experience. The amount you are pushed off course by the wind is known as 'leeway'.

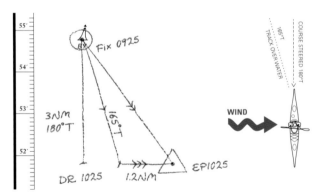

You allow for drift by simply adding or subtracting the estimated angle from the course steered. If you are being blown to the left of your course steered, subtract. If blown to the right, add.

Force (Bf)	wind speed (kt)	term	sea conditions	land conditions	paddling	speed with (kt)	speed against (kt)
Force 0	0	Calm	Mirror like.	Smoke rises vertically.	Easy paddling.	3	3
Force 1	1 – 3	Light air	Almost mirror like.	Smoke drifts with the wind, weather vanes do not move.	Easy paddling.	3	3
Force 2	4 – 6	Light breeze	Small wavelets. Crests of glassy appearance, not breaking.	Wind felt on face. Leaves rustle.	Easy paddling.	3	3
Force 3	7 – 10	Gentle breeze	Large wavelets. Crests begin to break; a few white horses.	Leaves and smaller twigs in constant motion. Light flags extended.	Relatively easy paddling. Noticeable work paddling into headwind. Novices start to struggle in cross-wind.	3.5	2.75
Force 4	11 – 16	Moderate breeze	Small waves, frequent white horses.	Dust, leaves and loose paper raised, Small branches begin to move.	Sustained effort into headwind. Following wind starts to become following sea.	3.5	2.75
Force 5	17 – 21	Fresh breeze	Moderate longer waves. Some foam and spray.	Small trees begin to sway.	Hard effort. Expect paddle flutter – begin to use low paddling style. Cross-winds become difficult.	3.75	2.5
Force 6	22 – 27	Strong breeze	Large waves with foam crests and some spray.	Large branches move. Whistling heard from overhead wires. Umbrella use becomes difficult.	Very hard effort. Paddle flutter requires control. Limit of practical paddling any distance into headwind. Following sea requires concentration.	4	2.25
Force 7	28 – 33	Moderate gale	Sea heaps up and foam begins to streak.	Whole trees in motion. Resistance felt when walking into the wind.	Strenuous. Following seas exhilarating for experienced paddler, but risk of capsize for inexperienced. Paddling across wind very difficult.	4.5	1.5
Force 8	34 – 40	Fresh gale	Moderately high waves with breaking crests forming spindrift. Streaks of foam.	Twigs broken from trees. Cars veer on road.	Very strenuous. Lots of concentration required downwind. Into the wind for only short distances (less than 0.5km).	4.5	1

Correcting for wind

Headwinds and tail winds are corrected for by simply increasing or decreasing your estimated speed.

Crosswinds using a transit

If you are travelling across a bay towards a headland, you may be able to line two objects up in a transit. To stay on your desired course over the ground you simply aim the boat as far left or right as it takes to stay on the transit.

Using a transit to correct for wind.

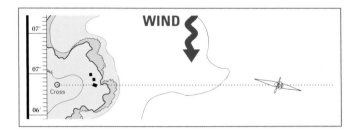

Crosswinds using a chart

With crosswinds you will need to:

1. Work out any tidal allowances first.

2. Estimate the number of degrees you will have to allow in order to compensate for the estimated drift.

3. Add or subtract this from the course to steer.

On page 73 after making allowance for tide the course to steer was 165°T. As you are about to set off a westerly breeze blows in and you decide to make an allowance of 15 degrees for drift.

Your original course to steer was 165°T. The wind is pushing you to the left (east), which means that in order to correct for drift you add 15 degrees to bring you back to the right. This means that your new course to steer is 180°T.

1   Using the rule of thirds, what is your drift between 0800 and 0900 if the max rate is
    4.5 knots and high water is at 1000?

2   Using a tidal diamond you find that the rate is 1 knot at 0835 and 1.6 knots at at 0935,
    what is your drift between 0835 and 0935?

3   Allowing for tide, using the diagram on page 70, assuming a drift of 1.5NM, what is
    your ground track expressed in degrees True?

4   Correcting for tide, using the diagram on page 71, assuming a drift of 1NM, what is
    your true course to steer?

5   If you are headed due north (000°) and the wind is a westerly:

    A   Would you add or subtract the 10° you decide
        to allow to compensate for the side wind?
    B   What course to steer would that give you in degrees True?

11 HANDHELD GPS

Familiarise yourself with your GPS unit before you use it on the water. The buttons will always be a little more fiddly when in a waterproof case.

GPS stands for Global Positioning System. Current systems provide worldwide cover and the most commonly used system relies on the American Navstar satellites. There is no doubt that the GPS is a fantastically useful tool, particularly when undertaking open sea crossings or when paddling in poor visibility. However, it is a tool in the same way as a compass – it makes navigation easier, but **you** are still the navigator; so don't throw away your compass and charts.

"NOTE: YOU SHOULD ALWAYS BE PREPARED AND CAPABLE OF NAVIGATING WITHOUT GPS. IT IS DESIGNED TO COMPLEMENT OTHER FORMS OF BASIC NAVIGATION, NOT ENTIRELY REPLACE THEM"

QUOTE FROM A GPS RECEIVER'S USER MANUAL

I tend to use a GPS when I need it, which is quite rarely, because most of the time I use 'eyeball navigation'. There is a view that you will never get the most out of your GPS unless you use it every time you go paddling. Either way it is important that you go out and practice using your GPS. You don't want to be thumbing through the instruction manual when you are shrouded in thick fog! So the first thing you need to do is work your way through the 'quick start guide' of the manual that comes with the GPS so that you are familiar with its controls and how to input information.

Manufacturers of GPS receivers (and sometimes different models from the same manufacturer) often use different terminology. As an example, what most textbooks call 'Cross Track Error' (see Chapter 12 Open Crossings) or XTE for short is referred to as 'off course' on the one I use. You will just have to wade through the manual and work it out.

Settings

As an example on my unit this is displayed as: H D° M.M' so that the position of my office is displayed as:

N 53° 08.591'
W 004° 16.526'

When you first use your GPS you will need to ensure that the basic settings are 'fit for purpose'. For use with nautical charts you would normally use:

Map datum: WGS 84

Position format: Hemisphere, Degrees, Minutes and portions of a minute expressed as a decimal value.

Distance/speed: Nautical miles and knots.

The convention as used on nautical charts would be written 53° 08'.6 N   4° 16'.5 W. You might say "fifty three degrees zero eight point six minutes north, four degrees sixteen point five minutes west." This is the format you would usually use when communicating with other vessels or the coastguard so that is the way I write them down no matter what format the GPS unit I use displays.

For normal purposes the position is rounded up to the nearest decimal place (tenths of a minute); in terms of latitude this would give you an accuracy of to within 200m (185.2m to be precise). In fog or at night you will probably want to work to 2 decimal places (hundredths of a minute), which would give you an accuracy of to within 20m. This would give the position as: 53° 08'.59 N   4° 16'.53 W.

If you are using a land map you will have to find out what the correct map datum setting is. For example if you are using British Ordnance Survey paper maps the settings would be:

OSGB on some receivers may be titled 'Maidenhead'.

Map datum: OSGB.

Position format: British grid reference.

Distance/speed: Metric (you may prefer to set this to nautical miles rather than convert tidal information into kilometres).

Direction: Decide whether you wish to read off bearings and courses as true or magnetic. It's a matter of personal preference.

WGS 84

The standard setting for GPS map datum is WGS 84 (World Geodetic Survey 1984). Maps (two-dimensional) can vary slightly in how they model the surface of the Earth (three-dimensional). As a result a standard datum was agreed for use with GPS. Unless the map you are using specifically indicates the use of a different map datum use WGS 84. Most new nautical charts comply with WGS 84. Some don't. If you have to use one that doesn't be aware that you have to make a small adjustment to the position indicated by the GPS before you plot the position on your chart. This is usually indicated clearly on the chart.

Position

These techniques have already been covered (pages 52 & 53). Consult your user manual to find out how your unit displays this information and how to enter a waypoint.

A GPS receiver can give your position in two ways:

1. As coordinates, e.g. latitude and longitude.

2. As a bearing and distance to a 'waypoint' which you have programmed into the GPS.

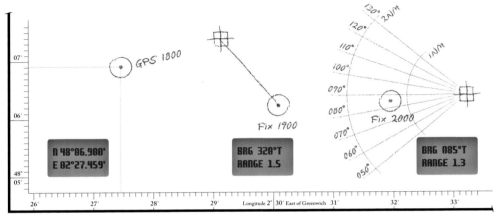

Position given as a coordinate GPS Fix (left) and as bearing and distance from a waypoint (centre).
Draw a 'spider's web' (right) around waypoints you are likely to approach often, to help you quickly mark a fix.

Handrailing

If you are following a featureless coast (low sand dunes, sand-banks and many similar looking channels between them) or a coast made featureless by poor visibility, you can use the latitude or longitude readout to tell you when to head in.

In the example illustrated the coast runs more north-south than east-west, so we use latitude (were it to run more east-west we would use longitude). The target is the farm at the road head which is on latitude 45° 34' N. As you are starting from Quicksand Creek 45° 30' N all you have to do is paddle on a rough bearing of 025°T, keep the land in sight on your left and turn onto a heading of 270°T when the GPS readout reaches the required latitude.

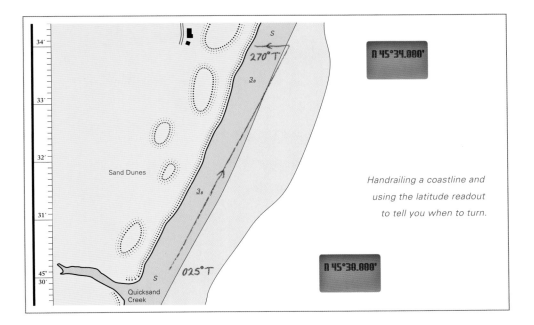

Handrailing a coastline and using the latitude readout to tell you when to turn.

ERRORS

Try not to become over-reliant on you GPS. Apart from the obvious potential for damage to delicate electronics in an unforgiving saltwater environment, there are many factors which can lead to inaccuracies: the signal's path through the ionosphere; Multi-Satellite Reception geometry; too few satellites within line of sight; or low battery power.

Very occasionally military tests designed to check the robustness of guidance systems will mean service is unavailable. (I jest not, warnings for specified areas appear in 'Notices to Mariners' provided by the UK Hydrographic Office on their website and announced by the coastguard over VHF radio).

The simplest and most likely cause of innacuracy is operator error (pushing the wrong buttons). Think how easy it is to dial a wrong number on the telephone.

So always do your best to plot an estimated position or back up your fix with visual bearings and transits. If your checks agree, then you can trust the GPS position and work your next EP from that. If they are radically different check for operator error!

Direction

GPS speak is slightly different from general navigational terminology. Terms which your GPS receiver may use are:

Bearing: the direction of a waypoint from your current position.

Course: the direction from one waypoint to another.

Heading: the direction in which you are pointing.

Course Over Ground (COG): the direction you are moving in.

Distance

When you select 'go to' the instrument will respond by indicating the bearing and the distance to the waypoint from your position.

Speed

The speed indicated on a GPS is your 'ground speed' (see page 68). Knowing your ground speed can be very useful.

Take care to set up the receiver to show speed averaged over several estimates of position. This is because small errors in current position compared with last position can result in the receiver displaying ridiculous instantaneous speed.

Average boat speed

As paddlers we have to 'guesstimate' our boat speed. However, when paddling on stretches of water that are not affected by tidal streams or winds, the ground speed and your boat speed will be the same. Record these readings and you will be able to build up a much more accurate picture of your true personal boat speed. This will significantly increase the accuracy of your estimates when planning crossings.

Tidal rate

In this way it is possible to use the GPS to identify areas of maximum tidal effect when paddling along a coastline. Moving to the left or the right may place you in a stronger stream resulting in more help from the tide.

There are many places where the tidal stream information available is 'sketchy' or even non-existent. If the tidal stream is running with or against you (and on coastal journeys it usually is) you can use your estimated boat speed and your known ground speed to work out what the tidal rate is. So if you estimate your boat speed at 3 knots and your GPS indicates a ground speed of 4.6 knots the tidal rate will be approximately 1.6 knots. This may allow you to plot a more accurate EP on your chart.

Putting waypoints into your GPS

There are a number of different ways to record waypoints in the memory of your GPS.

Record your position

'001' means nothing but 'bcrfbuoy' (my handset will only allow 8 letters or numbers – obviously refers to 'bone cruncher reef buoy'.

The simplest and most reliable way is to simply instruct the GPS to record your current position. So if you are visiting a place in good visibility and there is the possibility that you might wish to return there, simply press the appropriate button and then give the waypoint a meaningful name.

Manual input

Be wary of waypoints provided by nautical almanacs; they are usually much further out to sea than the coordinates we would choose for an approach. Use a chart and plot your own.

You can manually record a waypoint for any position. Whether planning a trip at the campsite or coping with changing conditions and plotting a new course from the deck of your kayak.

It is very tedious and time consuming inputting each individual letter and number of the waypoint's map reference. It is easy to insert a wrong character so it is **essential** that you compare the bearing and distance from your current position as plotted on a chart against the bearing and distance given by the GPS. If they don't match you have made a mistake.

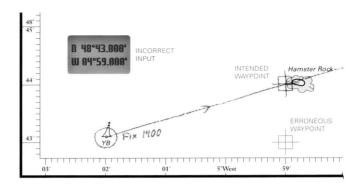

By comparing bearing and distance it is revealed that the figures entered are out by 1' of latitude which would put the position out by 1NM. Had the figures been out by 1° of latitude the waypoint would have been out by 60NM!

Using a computer

By far the easiest way to enter positions, waypoints and routes is to use a combination of mapping software, a computer, an interface connection and the receiver. GPS software for your PC is well worth the cash – you'll wonder why you didn't do it before!

GPS mapping software makes waypoint entry simpler, more visual and less prone to error. It can even be used on the water with expensive chart plotting handheld receivers. The obvious disadvantage is that it is only really suitable for route planning in advance of a journey. They are not a realistic option on multi-day trips where routes may need to be replotted several times; so it is important not to become reliant on them.

On the water

The simplest and most useful use of GPS receivers is to obtain a fix when you are uncertain of your position. You are then able to plot a new course to your destination. Provided there are no obvious discrepancies in your GPS fix you can trust the GPS in place of your estimated position, update your position and lay-off a new course (see also Chapter 12 Open Crossings).

SHAPING FOR EFFICIENCY

In any cross tide it is much more efficient to shape a course and use a course to steer than to follow the bearing given by the GPS.

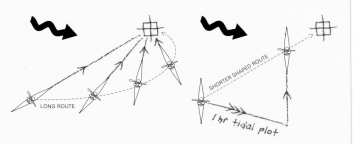

(Left) GPS doesn't allow for tide, you end up paddling further. (Right) by correcting for the tide and obtaining a course to steer you paddle a shorter route.

LONG ROUTE

SHORTER SHAPED ROUTE

1 hr tidal plot

Homing in

See Chapter 12 Open Crossings and Chapter 13 Poor Visibility for more on using waypoints.

Shaping a course will improve on your GPS based navigation where there are tidal streams. However in poor visibility a useful technique is to paddle your course to steer and then, when within 5 minutes of your ETA switch to the bearing supplied by the GPS and use it to 'home in' on your waypoint.

GPS INDUCED ACCIDENTS

There have been a number of cases where misusing GPS has caused boats to be wrecked. **GPS should always be used in conjunction with chart work**. Plot your waypoints and:

1. Compare bearing and distance to check that the figures entered into the receiver are correct.

2. Check that the course between each point doesn't lead you into danger.

3. Work out estimated positions and ground tracks in tidal areas.

Allowing for tide, this plot shows the GPS course of 083°T leads into the overfalls and rocks.

083°T

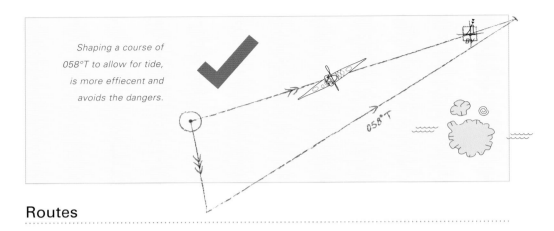

*Shaping a course of
058°T to allow for tide,
is more effiecent and
avoids the dangers.*

058°T

Routes

When you tell a GPS receiver to 'go to' a single waypoint it will
only supply you with a bearing to the waypoint from your current
position. As you move this bearing may change (see page 85).
When you link two waypoints to create a route the GPS can supply you with a course from Waypoint A to Waypoint B as well as a
bearing from your actual position to Waypoint B.

*Plot multiple waypoints on
your chart then transfer
them to your GPS.*

The best way to plan a route is to plot it on a chart, choosing
suitable features to navigate between. You would then make
waypoints for each of these features. By linking together these
waypoints you can create a route on your GPS.

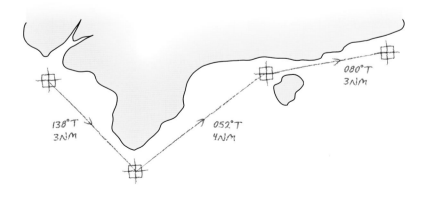

080°T
3NM

138°T
3NM

052°T
4NM

If you've set it up to do so, the GPS receiver will warn you when you are approaching your first waypoint and within a pre-set radius will automatically switch to the next waypoint, giving you the new course, bearing and distance.

Where there are tidal streams you will need to 'shape a course' on the chart to allow for their effect (see Chapters 10 and 12).

In areas unaffected by tidal streams you can simply follow the course supplied by the receiver. If you don't have to allow for wind or tide, course to steer and ground track are the same. But you should plot the course and distance on the chart anyway.

XTE

There is a useful function known as 'Cross Track Error' (XTE) that allows you to make adjustments to your course steered (or heading) to ensure that you stay on the course supplied by the GPS. In order to use XTE you have to define a line between your start position and your destination as a leg or stage of a route. Cross Track Error occurs when the path you take deviates to the left or right of your planned path and is indicated by the lateral distance from the chosen path.

Cross Track Error (XTE) function of a handheld GPS receiver.

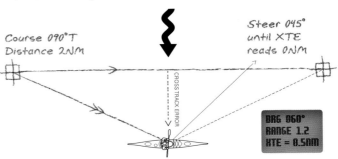

Knowing this you can make an adjustment to your course to get you back on your ground track. This is particularly useful when you are affected by a crosswind, as estimating leeway is notoriously difficult. In the example above the paddler makes a correction of 15° left of the bearing (060°) until back on the ground track.

XTE ferry glide

In poor visibility, XTE can be used instead of a transit. By experimenting with your course to eliminate Cross Track Error you perform a ferry glide along the ground track. Remember that this will only work if a cross tide is less than half your boat speed (see page 71). In places with strong tidal streams you will have to use the other techniques covered in Chapters 10 and 12.

Chart plotting GPS receivers

A plotter is a GPS receiver that incorporates an electronic map. Its main advantages are:

1. Waypoints are plotted visually using a cursor.

2. Your position is shown constantly in real time as you move over the map/chart.

3. Being very visual, it can be much more intuitive to use.

A compact chart plotting GPS receiver.

However plotters still don't allow for tide (although some of the sophisticated programmes available for laptops do!) and there are still the risks of failure and error; so you still need to do normal chart work. Another reason for still using charts is that a plotter screen is nowhere near as big as a chart. As you zoom out on an electronic map, less detail is displayed, so you may plot two waypoints at the magnification required to see them both and not see a danger between the two waypoints.

At the time of writing (2007), although small, battery operated, waterproof units are available, their screens are so small as to be of limited use. However, we can be confident that this will change in the near future.

GALILEO

In 2008 the European version of GPS (Galileo) will be operational. Unlike Navstar, which is a military system, Galileo is a civil system. Navstar is accurate (for civilians) to within 20m, whereas Galileo is planned to be accurate to 2m! From 2008 GPS receivers will be available that can use both systems.

EXERCISES

1 Plan a route using mapping software in a known safe environment; then put the route into practice by activating the route and following the instructions given.

2 Disobey a planned route by ignoring several waypoints, and then get back on track.

3 Reverse a route.

4 In good visibility, practice using the XTE function to perform a ferry glide across a short stretch of tidal water, without using transits.

12 OPEN CROSSINGS

When making a crossing where you have to allow for the tidal stream, there are a number of strategies that can be adopted. Some are simpler and some are more efficient than others.

Simple strategies

GPS

If using this tactic for a night crossing it would be a good idea to make a waypoint for your destination so that you can 'home in' on your target.

Slack water

If the crossing will only take twenty to thirty minutes, the simplest solution is to time your crossing so that it coincides with slack water. Ten to fifteen minutes either side of slack water the tidal stream will be either slack, or so weak that it poses no problem.

GPS

By inserting your start and finish point as waypoint in your GPS receiver and linking them as a route, you can use XTE to help you ferry glide even if you have no transits.

Ferry gliding

If the distance is relatively short, say up to 1.5 nautical miles, visibility good and the tidal stream running at half your boat speed or less, this is a viable no chart work option. Instead of pointing your boat in the direction of travel you point up into the tidal stream using a transit to help you judge how much allowance you have to make. The stronger the tidal stream the more you have to point into the tide and the longer the crossing will take.

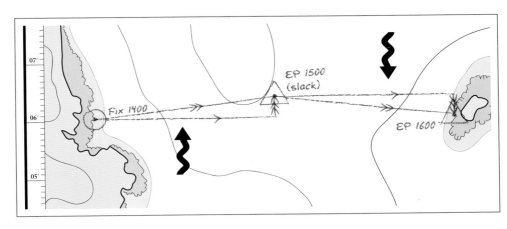

Timing

In most, but not all, places the tidal stream flows at similar rates in both directions. The trick is to time your passage so that for half of your journey the tide pushes you in one direction and for the other half it pushes you back again. In the figure above, the calculations would be made as follows:

GPS

In the above example XTE could be used to ensure that you stay on the desired ground track. To do this you would have to create three waypoints: A, EP 1500 and B.

```
Distance A-B = 6NM          Start = 1400
Speed = 3kn                 Slack water = 1500
Time taken = 2 hours        Finish = 1600
```

Plot your projected EPs and ground track so that if a change of plan calls for it, your rough position is known throughout.

Correcting for tide over more than an hour

If timings are not so simple, corrections may have to be made for the effect of the tidal stream. In Chapter 10 we looked at how to correct for tide by 'shaping a course' over a one hour period, steering a different course to the desired ground track. Here, we'll look at longer crossings.

GPS

The advantage of this method is that your ground track remains constant. So you would only need to enter two waypoints (the headland and island) to be able to use XTE.

Longer way

Correcting for the tidal stream on an hour by hour basis may lead you to paddle further than necessary. This is because some of the corrections may have cancelled eachother out over the period of the whole journey. Over several hours this can add up to a good deal of wasted effort. You also have to change course to steer every hour.

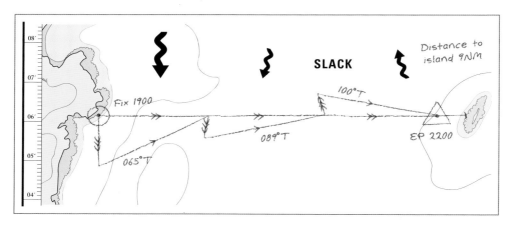

Shorter way

This involves working out roughly how long the journey will take and then plotting the tidal movement over the whole of that period (in this case three hours) before plotting the course to steer.

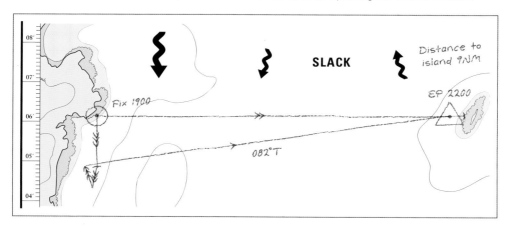

GPS

By entering the start point, the projected EPs and the finish point as waypoints and linking them as a route you will be able to use XTE.

This method saves physical effort (note the position at EP2200) and your course to steer throughout the crossing remains the same. The downside is that if you wish to know your actual position at any given time (a change of plan forced on you by changing conditions would require this) you will need to plot projected EPs (allowing rather than correcting for tide) for each hour.

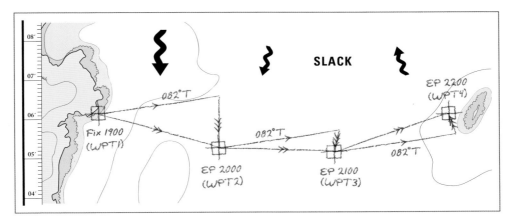

Working the tide

In all the previous examples the assumption has been that you are starting your journey at the point where the crossing is at its narrowest. If however you are starting from a point further along the coast you can make even more effective use of the tide.

1. Work out how long it would take to complete the crossing if there were no tidal streams, in this case two hours.

2. Plot an estimated position a little upstream of the target to allow a margin for error. If your calculations are spot on you simply stop paddling and allow the tide to sweep you towards the island. If you are slightly slower than expected you will still be on target.

3. Plot the tidal stream over the travel period in question, working backwards. This example starts with the tidal drift between 1300 and 1400, and finishes with the drift from 1200 to 1300.

4. Plot a compass course that takes you from the mainland to the end of the tidal allowance at right angles to the tidal stream.

All you have to do is ensure that you set off from this point at the right time, in this case 1200 hours.

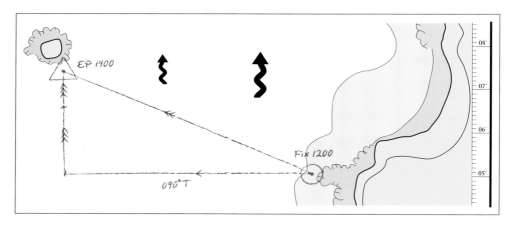

GPS

By plotting EPs and entering the start point, the projected EPs and the finish point as waypoints and linking them as a route you will be able to use XTE.

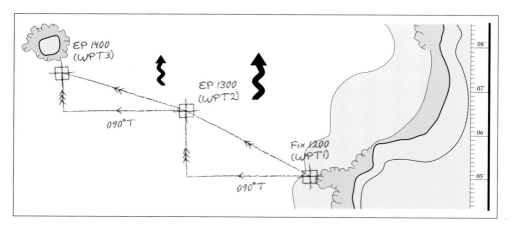

1. On a short crossing of 1NM with the tidal stream running at a maximum speed of 1 knot, it would be reasonable to use a transit to perform a ferry glide. True or false?

2. If in the example opposite, the tidal drift was 3NM for the first hour and 4NM for the second hour, how far upstream (south) would you have to set off (assuming a boat speed of 3 knots) in order to 'drift' onto the island?

3. The south-going stream begins at 1134 in the example on page 91. What time would you set off?

4. Using the example at the bottom of page 92, work out the course to steer, assuming a boat speed of 3 knots and the following sets and drifts:

1900 – 2000	180°	1NM
2000 – 2100	000°	1.5NM
2100 – 2200	000°	0.5NM

13 POOR VISIBILITY

Above ~ Sea fog blowing in.

The navigational techniques used in heat haze, fog or at night are no different to those we have already covered. What may change is the way you deploy them.

Preparation

Night exercise, circa 1984.

In good visibility there are usually a number of options available; so if you forget a piece of information or an item of equipment you can usually cope. In poor visibility you will need all the help you can get; so it is essential that you are meticulous in your planning.

Training

Having to navigate in poor visibility can be very stressful. It pays to practise all the techniques you are likely to need in good visibility until you are thoroughly familiar with them. Then go out at night and practise your navigational skills in a relatively safe environment (such as an enclosed bay or a quiet harbour).

Navigational information

Keep all the information you may need to hand. Work out the range of figures for period afloat and make sure that there is more than one copy of this information between the group.

Study the charts to learn which lights you are likely to be able to identify and highlight them on the chart. Make sure you clearly understand their colours, timing and sequences.

Equipment

At night, temperatures drop, so wear plenty of clothing.

Make sure that every member of the group has at least two sources of lighting. Every paddler should have a waterproof head torch and a light stick attached to the shoulder strap of their buoyancy aid (or better still, on top of a hat). The navigator should carry two waterproof torches.

Better still, attach the light stick to the top of your hat, if worn.

- Waterproof head torch, versatile and hands free.

- Light stick, attached to bouyancy aid shoulder strap as a marker.

- Whistle, to signal presence/position to the group in darkness.

- Personal flare (red pinpoint) in case of separation from the group.

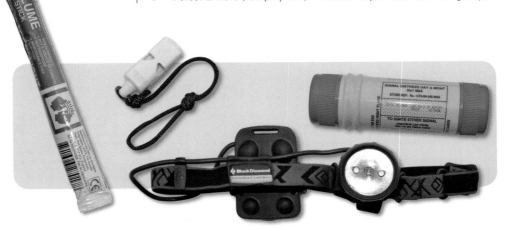

Night vision

Those not navigating should keep their torches off. The light sticks will not affect their night vision and they will be able to spot features much further away to alert the navigator.

It can take five to ten minutes for good night vision to return after exposure to bright white light such as the navigator will have to use to read the chart. You can reduce the intensity by covering the torch glass in gaffer tape and making a small hole in the tape that lets out just enough light to read the chart by.

Useful tactics

Short legs

Try and keep the distances between identifiable features on your route as short as possible. If you are 10% out on a 300m leg your target will be 30m away and you may be able to pick it out at night. On a 1km leg you might be a 100m out and lose the target.

There will be occasions where this is not an option for safety reasons, for example waves breaking onshore.

Use handrails

Following a handrail is a surer way to find your target. In poor visibility it may be better to take a slightly longer but more certain route to the next target.

Aim off

If your target is on a featureless coast, you can find the coastline and follow it to the target. By deliberately aiming off to one side you can be sure of which way to turn when you meet the shore.

Aiming off to the east onto a sandy shore, then turning left along the shore to find the track.

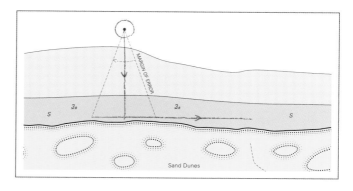

Choose big targets

If you have to follow a compass bearing, try and choose targets that are large and/or well lit. That way even if you are a bit out it will be easy to see the target.

Attack points

If your final location is difficult to identify, go to a nearby 'big target' first. You can then use the 'big target' as an attack point from which to find the smaller target.

Plotting a course to the headland, sets up an 'attack point' from which to find the smaller island.

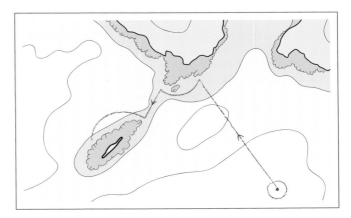

Extended line

When approaching a small feature at the end of a long leg you can increase the group's range of vision by getting them to paddle in line abreast to either side of the navigator.

Take care to ensure the group does not get split up. When the target is found the paddlers on the end of the line move towards whoever has found the target, collecting the other paddlers as they go.

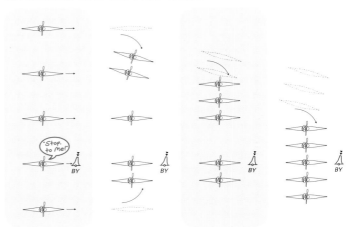

GPS & poor visibility

GPS is both useful and reassuring in poor visibility. If a night paddle is planned, work out your route and enter all the waypoints before you set off.

Organisation & leadership

Most sea kayakers are happy to leave the navigation to someone else. It is therefore absolutely critical that a group paddling in poor visibility does not get split up.

Leadership

In good conditions it is not unusual for groups of friends to take a very laid back approach to group control. At night this could prove disastrous. Like it or not, someone will have to take control and offer a more formal approach to group control. The group will have to be clearly organised and briefed about their responsibilities.

Group control

The group must be briefed on the importance of sticking like glue to the navigator.

At night it is a good idea for the navigator, or whoever is appointed to steer the compass or GPS course, to wear a different coloured light stick to everyone else.

Divide the group into pairs of buddies. In addition to having a responsibility to the whole group, each paddler will be particularly responsible for their buddy. So if someone is busy sorting something out and hasn't noticed that the group are setting off, their buddy will ask the group to stop.

If the group is large it may be worth getting everyone to 'number off' in a quick roll call. The leader shouts 'One', the next paddler shouts 'Two' and so on, until you either reach the number of people in the group or someone is found to be missing.

Communication

Sound signals should be agreed by the group. You will probably only need two. I suggest the following:

1. Continuous short whistle blasts. Meaning: "I'm in trouble/lost" (given by whoever is in trouble).

2. One long whistle blast, repeated after a pause if necessary. Meaning: "Regroup on me" (only to be used by leader).

EXERCISES

1   Plan a route in a relatively enclosed safe area. Enter the features you plan to paddle to as waypoints in your GPS receiver and link them as a route.

2   Paddle the route at night using your GPS.

3   Paddle the route again using only compass and chart.

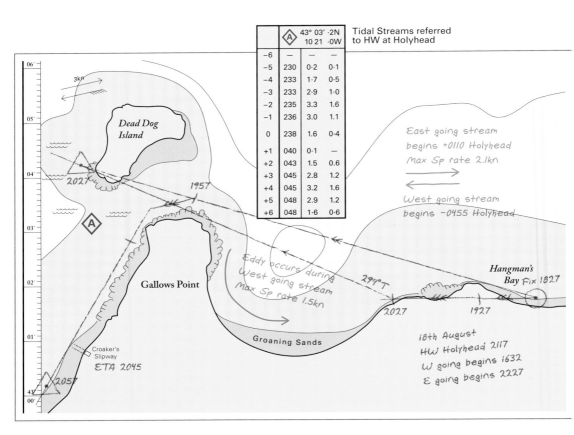

	43° 03' ·2N 10 21 ·0W	Tidal Streams referred to HW at Holyhead	
-6	—	—	—
-5	230	0·2	0·1
-4	233	1·7	0·5
-3	233	2·9	1·0
-2	235	3·3	1·6
-1	236	3·0	1·1
0	238	1·6	0·4
+1	040	0·1	—
+2	043	1·5	0·6
+3	045	2·8	1·2
+4	045	3·2	1·6
+5	048	2·9	1·2
+6	048	1·6	0·6

Dead Dog Island

3kn

2027

1957

East going stream begins +0110 Holyhead Max Sp rate 2.1kn

West going stream begins −0455 Holyhead

Ⓐ

Gallows Point

Eddy occurs during West going stream Max Sp rate 1.5kn

294°T

Hangman's Bay Fix 1827

2027

1927

Groaning Sands

2027

18th August
HW Holyhead 2117
W going begins 1632
E going begins 2227

Croaker's Slipway

ETA 2045

2057

14 PLANNING A TRIP

You could even test the accuracy of your plan, travel out to a key location and watch the tide turn.

If you have diligently worked your way through this book you already have all the knowledge you need to find the right information to plan a trip. There is nothing wrong with planning your trip on the back of an envelope. However, by working through the planning sheet provided you will ensure that you don't miss out a vital stage.

You can adapt the trip planner opposite or download an A4 version from the resources area at www. pesdapress.com/printables.

Passage planning is fine as long as you can keep to your timings. If a change of plan is needed it is as well to have the information readily to hand. Laminate the Planning Sheet and fill in the details so that you can use it again and for repeated trips.

TRIP PLANNER

For further guidance on the use of this planner refer to the example in *Sea Kayak Navigation* (second edition) or visit *www.pesdapress.com*/articles.

Pesda Press LTD

from	Hangman's Bay	to	Croaker's Slipway
date	18th August	local time	BST (GMT +0100)

convert all times to local times

WEATHER FORECAST

wind	SE 2-3	weather	Sunny spells, occ. showers
visibility	Good	sea state	Slight. Mod where exposed to W swell

TIDES

HW standard port	Liverpool 2205	other tidal ports	
conversion	-0048		
HW secondary port	Holyhead 2117		
tidal range	6.7m		
phase	Halfway between SP and NP		

NAVIGATION

group	Competent/strong	variation	5°W
estimated speed	3 knots	total distance	13NM
ETD	1827	time by DR	4 hr 20 min
ETA (allowing for tide)	2045	time allowing for tide	2 hr 18 min

outline

Paddle on 294°T to stay in the main tide and avoid the eddy.
As soon as slipway shows, paddle close to shore to stay out of the overfalls.

escape points	Groaning Sands		

TIDAL INFORMATION

Between Hangman's Bay & Gallows Point

HW Hhd	2117
W-going begins	-0445
	1632

Drift (from rule of thirds):

1627	0.5
1727	1.0
1827	1.5
1927	1.5 } W-going
2027	1.0
2127	0.5
2227	0.5 } E-going
2327	

HW Hhd	2117
E-going begins	+0110
	2227

Max SP rate	2.1 knots
Max rate expected	1.5 knots

Ⓐ

1917	235°	2.4kn
2017	236°	2kn
2117	238°	1kn
2217	040°	—

On the chart, the first leg vector is worked out over two hours, between 1827 and 2027. We need to change course three quarters of the way along the water track. The water track was calculated over 2 hours so we have to change course after 1 hour 30 minutes, which gives us a time of 1957.

FOR THE MATHEMATICALLY MINDED

The average speed, (worked out by measuring the ground track and dividing it by time taken), is 8.2 divided by 2 hours = 4.1 knots. We need to change course after 6.2NM.

$$\frac{Distance}{Speed} = Time \qquad \frac{6.2}{4.1} = 1.5 \ (one \ and \ a \ half \ hours) \qquad 1827 + 0130 = 1957$$

On the second leg we have made the assumption that, given the shape of the land, the tidal stream will not go in exactly the same direction as in the middle of the sound. It will probably 'set in' and follow the coastline. It will also probably not be as powerful as it is in the middle of Dead Dog Sound. So we have decided to only allow 1.5 knots of tide with us rather than the just over 2 indicated by using the data provided by tidal diamond A. By plotting a course that follows the land and allowing 1.5NM for drift and 3NM for our speed over one hour we end up with an EP for 2057 that is a little further on than our destination. It is roughly 4/5 of the ground track over one hour which equates to 48 minutes. So our ETA is 1957 + 0048 = 2045.

FOR THE MATHEMATICALLY MINDED

Speed is 3 knots plus 1.5 knots = 4.5 knots. Distance from change of course to Croaker's Slipway is 3.6NM.

$$\frac{3.6}{4.5} = 0.8 \ of \ one \ hour = 48 \ minutes.$$

There is no real need to use such accurate chart work for this trip. You could set off any time after 1800 secure in the knowledge that the tide would push you along nicely, and that it would take a lot less than the 4 hours 20 minutes. However, it is best to practise this level of accuracy before setting out on trips that demand it.

NOW IT IS TIME TO GET OUT THERE AND DO IT. GOOD PADDLING!

EXERCISES

Read the advice in the introduction! Then volunteer to do the planning for a trip that someone else is leading and get the leader to check your planning.

Plan a trip of your own and get someone else to plan the same trip. Compare results. If they are not reasonably close work out between you what the mistakes are. Paddle the planned trip and compare your planning with what actually happens.

INDEX

This is where the Adventure starts..

Now you know where you are going, get the equipment to get you back

Mail Order hotline +44 (0) 161 474 1499

canoes and **kayaks** .co.uk

Photo: Curtis Byrne. Location: Alaska

DESPERATE
MEASURES

At the heart of British sea Kayaking

Did you know that we're on the doorstep of two of the largest sea kayak manufacturers in the world? Visit our Nottingham showroom for advice, demos, accessories, service and choice.

VALLEY THE ORIGINAL BRITISH SEA KAYAK **P.H** *+MORE*

designed
so you can stay in control

TEMPEST: Everything about Tempest was designed for days like this; a well mannered hull that amplifies your skills and minimizes mistakes, ultra-comfortable cockpit, and meticulous outfitting. A combination of solid initial stability and strong tracking even in high winds make the Tempest an excellent choice for calm or rough-water expedition paddling. Take the ride of your life in a Tempest.

THE COMPLETE TEMPEST FAMILY: 165, 165 Pro, 170, 170 Pro and 180 Pro

WILDERNESS
SYSTEMS